Customer-Friendly:
Design Guidelines for E-Commerce

About the Author

Dr Joseph Feller teaches e-commerce strategy, design, and development for the Department of Accounting, Finance and Information Systems, University College Cork. He formerly lectured at the Ringling School of Art and Design in Florida, and is an experienced consultant in the areas of internet strategy and customer-centred design.

Customer-Friendly: Design Guidelines for E-Commerce

Joseph Feller

Department of Accounting, Finance and
Information Systems
University College Cork
Ireland

BLACKHALL
Publishing

This book was typeset by Artwerk for

Blackhall Publishing,
8 Priory Hall, Stillorgan,
Co. Dublin,
Ireland.

Email: blackhall@eircom.net
Website: www.blackhallpublishing.com

A catalogue record for this book is available from the British Library

ISBN: 1 842180 11 8

Printed in Ireland by
ColourBooks Ltd

Dedication

This book is dedicated to Carol, Caelen and Bean.

Contents

Preface

I wrote this book with three goals:

- to get e-commerce decision-makers, from company CEOs down to the summer interns, excited about, and committed to, customer-friendly web design
- to teach the basic principles of building websites that are fast, flexible, and easy to use
- to highlight specific techniques for building the components of a dynamic, value packed, commercial web environment.

There are two intended audiences for this book. First and foremost are the professionals who are shaping e-commerce today — the strategists, architects, visual designers and programmers building web environments. Although much of the material in the book is focused on development, it is not a book about technology. (For readers unfamiliar with some of the technological jargon, there is a glossary at the end of the book.) Secondly, this book was written for the e-commerce professionals of tomorrow — students (like my own) in business programmes, information systems and computer science departments, in fact anyone training to meet the needs of a growing market that demands powerful, useful and painless technology.

The first four chapters of the book deal with basic principles. They discuss:

- the need for more customer-friendly design
- the ways in which the design process can facilitate a customer-friendly end product
- the enormous importance of content
- the three pillars of better web design — speed, flexibility and usability.

Chapters 5 to 8 look at some key aspects of any commercial web site, including navigation and search systems, purchasing mechanisms and community design. The book is supported by a website at http://www.blackhallpublishing.com/customer-friendly. The website contains a portal to online and offline resources related to customer-friendly design, customer-friendly design tips and commercial website critiques (all frequently updated). There is also a forum to which readers can submit their own tips and critiques. I hope that you make use of it. Please feel free to contact me directly at jfeller@afis.ucc.ie.

Disclaimers

This book contains many design critiques, many of them negative (though, I feel, fair). All of these critiques should be read in the constructive spirit in which they were intended. Readers who disagree with the observations made are encouraged to visit the website to speak their minds.

The web is a volatile medium and sites change quickly. Many of the screen captures in this book reflect sites that only exist now in memory or archives. In fact, in trying to grab better images, I noticed that many of the sites had been significantly redesigned since I had last visited, and mainly for the better.

CHAPTER 1:

The Death of the Inconvenience Store

Online, you win with a good experience. Not the ads, not the hype marketing, not the glitzy technology, not the cute logo, not the IPO price ...or even the very nice sushi you served at your last party. It's the customer experience, stupid. What happens when visitors come to your site and the site sucks? Will you eat your sushi then?

Mark Hurst, President of Creative Good (Hurst, 2000)

The Case for Better Design

E-commerce is the creation and exchange of value through the use of information and communication technology (ICT). The design challenge of e-commerce is to build online environments which will make possible this creation and exchange of value.

E-commerce comes in many shapes and sizes but, in general, a line can be drawn between *organisational e-commerce* (sometimes called e-business) and *consumer e-commerce*. Organisational e-commerce can take place *within* a company (e.g. delivering online training through an intranet or creating virtual workspaces) or *between* companies (e.g. automating document exchange between companies or transferring funds online). In contrast, consumer e-commerce steps outside the organisation and into the mass market. In some cases, the internet is used to connect companies to consumers — for example, in an online retail outlet. In other cases, it is used to connect consumers to consumers — for example, in an online auction house.

This book offers guidelines on how to use one particular technology, namely the world wide web (WWW or web), to build better consumer e-commerce environments. This is not to suggest that the web is the best the world of ICT has to offer, nor that consumer activity is somehow more important than organisational activity. As a matter of fact, consumer e-commerce is (and will continue to be) dwarfed by organisational e-commerce; by some estimates, consumer activity accounts for only 10% of the e-economy (Tedeschi, 1999c). However, from the point of view of learning good design, consumer e-commerce offers two advantages — portability and dramatically demonstrated need.

The US Army often trains medics in the emergency rooms of big city hospitals. Why? Because it is in this environment that they are most likely to gain experience treating violent injuries in the chaos of triage. By choosing to focus on consumer design, I am following the same logic. The lessons learned in the process of designing websites for consumer audiences are applicable everywhere, but cannot be easily learned anywhere else. For example, three of the unquestionable challenges of commercial web design — speed, flexibility and usability — are often understated in organisational projects. While most home-users have slow and expensive internet connections, business users (of an intranet for example) enjoy rapid network access. Thus the need for speed is often overlooked. Likewise, customers visit e-commerce websites using a wide range of software and hardware. And yet designers must ensure that all users have access to a complete and well designed experience. In organisational e-commerce, where the end-user technology is centrally controlled, this sensitivity to the means of consumption is often underdeveloped. Finally, consumer sites must be easy to learn and easy to use, if companies are to have any hope of turning shoppers into buyers and, more importantly, into long-term return visitors. In business environments, usability issues are often downplayed since corporate users are *required* to learn, use and reuse the system as part of their job.

These challenges are, of course, not unique to the consumer web. That's exactly the point. Organisational e-commerce sites should also be faster, more flexible and more usable. But these are all design skills best gained in the trenches of consumer e-commerce where there are radical differences between users, tremendous variations in technology and access speeds, and where the competition is always just a click.away.

So much for portability. The second compelling reason for focusing on consumer e-commerce is need: dramatic, in-your-face, daily demonstrated need. Consumer e-commerce is suffering from ease of access. Both dotcoms and bricks-and-mortar companies seeking to do business online are finding it easier and easier to do so. This low barrier of entry has led to an emphasis on speed and hype over quality. Even the most successful companies are vulnerable to bad design. In early 1999 the most popular feature on the IBM corporate website was the 'Search' function because users found the navigational system too difficult to use. Sadly, the second most popular feature was the 'Help' function because the 'Search' mechanism was not much better. In response to these problems, IBM devoted considerable resources to redesigning the site. The results were astounding: in a single week, use of the 'Help' function decreased 84%. More importantly, in that same week, sales increased 400% (Tedeschi, 1999a). As if to drive home the point, when Jakob Nielsen (1999) reviewed the sites of ten major corporations, the redesigned IBM site ranked highest in terms of speed and usability.

This anecdote dramatically demonstrates the relationship between website design and sales — a relationship that is also evident in the wider e-marketplace. Research company Creative Good reports that four out of every ten customers grow frustrated with the web stores they are using and move to alternative, offline, shopping venues (Hurst and Gellady, 1999). It's not really surprising. When commercial sites are slow and hard to use, e-commerce loses the appeal of convenience. When customers can't find products, they certainly can't buy them. And when users are barraged with JavaScript error messages, or when pages come out half-baked, it makes it difficult to establish the trust needed to conduct a transaction.

These examples certainly do not suggest that a well designed website will guarantee success in e-commerce. The IBM experience, after all, was the result of decades of effort spent establishing a global brand and an eager, loyal customer base. However, poor website design may be all that is needed to guarantee failure. If Creative Good's research is accurate, nearly half of all consumer e-commerce revenues are lost to poor design.

I remember a 'Far Side' cartoon by Gary Larson that showed a little boy straining to retrieve a product from a store shelf, straining because the lowest shelf was at ceiling height. The caption read: 'Inconvenience Stores'. To any web shopper, it is obvious that the chaotic race to establish an internet presence, without regard to quality, has resulted in an online marketplace glutted with such inconvenience stores. It should be just as obvious to businesses that to succeed in the consumer electronic arena, design must become a fundamental part of strategy, and vice versa. Why? Because a poorly designed site can undo even the most successful business. No-one would look at the IBM experience and say that sales went up because the new and improved website somehow quintupled demand. The demand was already there. The reality is that the original website was so poorly designed that 80% of eager-to-buy customers were forced to go elsewhere for their purchases.

The Basics of Customer-Friendly Design

To repeat, an e-commerce website is an environment for creating and exchanging value. (Note that from this point on, the term e-commerce refers to *consumer e-commerce*.) A website looks like a publication, but it's not. It feels like a computer application, but it's not. It is both these things — and more. For the most common consumer business model, which is some sort of retail, the bottom line is that an e-commerce website is a store. It is not an 'alternative' sales channel. It is a *primary* channel. And designing such an environment is as complex a process as building a physical store, perhaps more so.

Welcome to the e-commerce universe. Here, in the centre, you'll find the root of it all. No, not TCP/IP, not SSL, not fibre-optics, but the customer. Successful e-commerce sites are customer-friendly. This means e-commerce professionals must seek to view the web from the customer's point of view. But what is this point of view? It is a view that sees all web stores as complete, stand-alone shopping environments. For the duration of the visit, what sits in the user's browser is the sole interface between the company and the customer. If the interface does not provide a valuable service to the customer — that is, good information, a pleasant experience, etc. — then the product line, the pricing scheme and the post-sales service won't really matter. A poor environment will stop customers dead in their tracks.

Web designers have traditionally based their activities on the experiences of print designers and application developers. But as noted above, an e-commerce site is more than just a publication or an application. In a world of new media, new economics and new rules, it sometimes pays to learn from the old. The bottom line is that e-commerce designers have a lot to gain from a visit to the shopping mall. What's the first thing you do on an offline shopping trip? Navigate traffic and find a parking space. Strange as it may sound, location and parking facilities are the first opportunities for an offline vendor to deliver, or fail to deliver, value to a customer. A customer who is forced to circle around for twenty minutes or more will enter the store in a foul humour, if at all. Parking is problematic for two reasons: space is limited and space is shared. For the retailer, the challenge is to get the customer to the store in a quick and painless manner. For the e-tailer, the challenge is to get the store to the customer. Network congestion has replaced traffic gridlock and messages that the server is down or not responding now take the place of overflowing parking lots. The terminology has changed but the problems remain the same. Bandwidth, like physical space, is limited and shared.

Customer-friendly design calls for attention to exactly this kind of detail. Designers need to ask themselves:

- is my online parking lot delivering value
- does my server architecture resemble a six-storey garage or six curbside spaces
- do my customers need to 'drive' a particular browser or have a particular plug-in in order to park
- how long do my customers have to wait just to get into the store?

Likewise, designers don't usually think about web design as a human resource activity, but it is. Every line of copy, every graphic, every link, every SQL query or pop-up window acts as a customer service representative. A major part of e-commerce design is recruiting and training this virtual staff. Spend a day shopping online and the sad truth comes out — too many web stores are filled with lazy, rude and ignorant employees. They give customers the wrong information, lead them down the wrong aisle or, worst of all, fail to interact with customers at all.

The customer-friendly designer must make certain that staff are well trained. When customers decide they want to learn more about a particular product, can every page of the site tell them where the item is located, or at least get them to the right area of the store? Can the 'sales staff' offer solid advice to help customers choose between products, or do they just spout marketing copy? Are they capable of listening, and reacting, to customer feedback? Does every page provide customers with an accessible explanation regarding privacy and security? Or does the virtual sales team just offer 'trust us' as an assurance of legitimacy? Offline, a store's staff plays many roles — to extend a friendly greeting, to guide customers around the store, to offer informed advice about products, to explain store policies and to listen to complaints. Online, the site is the staff and must play all of these roles.

Customers want convenience, which means fast, easy-to-use sites that won't crash their computers. But customers don't go to an e-commerce site to experience these things. They go to shop. Everywhere I look, I see sites that have been optimised for a particular screen resolution, a particular modem speed or a particular browser. What are really needed are web stores that have been optimised for shopping. Sometimes customers are making a planned purchase. *Planned purchasing* is the process of wish fulfilment and the job of the site is to help customers find products that they already know they want. Other times, customers are making impulse purchases. Impulse shopping is the process of wish creation and the job of the site is to introduce customers to new products and services.

A customer-friendly site supports both modes of shopping. To support planned shopping, the site must be flexible enough to handle the real world of human navigation. Every customer has a different way of categorising products; one may view Disney's *Dumbo* as a video, another as a children's product. A customer-friendly site allows both these customers to find their way. Customers should be spending their time sifting through wonderful products to buy and not through ambiguous navigation labels. To support impulse shopping, product offers must be both appropriate and value-added. For example, on one online shopping trip for a telescope tripod, the dynamically generated check-out page included a link to a set of lens filters with a discount. The offer made sense. I was buying a telescope accessory, so enticing me to buy a telescope (which presumably I already owned) would have been, frankly, stupid. But by offering me other accessories — and at a discount — the site treated me just as a clever and courteous salesperson would. I followed the link. Customer-friendly sites are personalised and knowledgeable, and they give customers incentives to add another wish — and purchase — to their list.

Customer-friendly sites are also accurate — dead accurate. Offline, customers often tolerate advertisements that can't be fulfilled and shelf displays of out-of-stock items. But online, where they often wait not only for the page to load, but also for a database to build the page, customers demand accuracy. Online, the stockroom is the store. There should be no mistakes, no 'checking in the back'. Likewise, customer-friendly sites don't tease customers. They deliver. I'm a registered user at Amazon.co.uk. I subscribe to seven of their newsletters, explicitly indicating my reading interests. But I've never purchased anything. When I visit the site, the customised front page says 'Welcome back Joseph Feller, we have recommendations for you'. But when I follow the link, I see 'Based on your purchases we're still not sure of your tastes. Check back after you've ordered again. We'll make suggestions when we have a better idea of what you might enjoy.' Amazon is a market leader and should know better. If my seven category choices don't give Amazon an 'idea' of what I might enjoy, what will? Customer-friendly sites don't lead shoppers down dead ends and they don't promise content that is not there. The cutting edge of the commercial web is not delivering multimedia — it is delivering customised, accurate information.

Finally, while getting into an online store should be easy, and moving around and finding products and information should be easier, getting out should be the easiest of all. And yet it is often the most difficult part of the e-shopping trip. Confusing, inflexible, inefficient and overly intrusive check-out mechanisms have led to many an abandoned shopping cart in cyberspace. Customer-friendly sites offer a speedy, courteous and simple set of tools to complete the purchase. After all, the goal of a retail site is to get people to buy things. Once they do, it's suicide to penalise them for it.

A commitment to customer-friendly design comes in two phases. First, there is the realisation that e-commerce design is closer to architecture than to graphic design or even software engineering. It is the act of building an environment. Second, there is the realisation that the user of the environment — the customer — must be the impetus and final test of every design decision. E-commerce designers are building parking lots, training sales staff, stocking shelves, dressing window displays, automating inventory management and trying to reward customers for buying. The challenge is considerable.

In a nutshell, customer-friendly design:

- identifies customers and their needs and desires
- treats customers as individuals and provides content and functionality to address their needs and desires
- provides a positive, value-creating experience.

It is telling (and encouraging) that a number of major design firms now advertise themselves as creators and shapers, not of websites, but of customer experiences. Creative Good's president Mark Hurst has argued time and again that 'the key driver of success for any online store is the customer experience' (Hurst, 1999). Likewise, the Viant Design Studio describes their methodology, Experience

Architecture, as 'a user-centred approach to interactive design that achieves business goals by meeting user goals' (Viant Design Studio, 1999).

Overview of the Design Process

Webreview, an online magazine for web developers, describes itself as providing 'cross training for web teams'. Anyone involved with the web knows that this is not just a catchy slogan, it's a way of life. To work within the unique characteristics, capabilities and limitations of the web, an e-commerce development team must draw upon a variety of strategic, technological and creative disciplines. To be effective, these diverse skills need to be co-ordinated in a well defined design process. Jennifer Fleming (1998) has pointed out that although every design team's process is unique, the industry has adopted a fairly 'consistent vision' of the main stages of the web development lifecycle. These stages are:

1. Information gathering.
2. Strategy.
3. Prototyping.
4. Implementation.
5. Launch.
6. Maintenance and growth.

Fleming's six-stage approach is derived from the world of software development. It is similar to the traditional 'waterfall' approach of information systems building, which has been described as the process of:

- deciding what is to be done
- deciding how to do it
- doing it
- testing it
- using it (Bahrami, 1999).

The rest of this section offers a brief summary of the activities and skills involved in each of these six stages, with a focus on making the process more customer-friendly.

The first two stages — information gathering and strategy — form the basis of the entire development project. Strangely, the e-commerce industry has, for the most part, viewed these stages as somehow unrelated to design. Research and strategy, the conventional wisdom goes, is for marketers, business developers and top management. But, as we've seen, to build a customer-friendly site, the needs of customers must be addressed from the starting line. From this perspective, the primary goals of a company at these stages should be to:

- understand *who* will use the site
- understand *how* they will use the site
- determine what *functionality* they will need to use the site
- determine what *content* they will need to use the site.

Based on this customer-centred information gathering process, the company will be able to:

- articulate the business plan and project goals
- understand the competition
- determine the most effective promotional strategies
- determine a suitable technological platform for delivering the site's content
- determine project needs and allocate resources.

There are many excellent books on the market which focus on e-commerce business models and strategy building. A good place to start is with *BLUR: The Speed of Change in the Connected Economy* (Davis and Meyer, 1998) and *Information Rules: A Strategic Guide to the Network Economy* (Shapiro and Varian, 1999).

To add to this literature, I would offer companies the following advice:

- make the first goal in the business plan the creation of an online environment that is easy and pleasant to use and that facilitates the creation and exchange of value
- appoint an individual or group to act as the 'customer interface' watchdog
- make certain that everyone involved in the project understands that customer-friendly design is a fundamental criteria for success.

If a company can secure top level commitment to customer-friendly design and ensure that everyone, from marketing to the server administrator, is taking the customer into account, then it is well on its way. In terms of design, there are two disciplines that should be spotlighted, as they are crucial to the information/strategy phase of the project: use-case modelling and information architecture.

Use-case modelling

Use-case modelling is a technique widely used in object-oriented systems development. It was pioneered by Ivar Jacobson. In a nutshell, use-case modelling is a method for determining the functional requirements of a system by identifying:

- different users and classes of users
- the roles that they play
- the scenarios in which they interact with the system and with each other (Bahrami, 1999).

Use-case modelling has much to offer developers of e-commerce sites because it allows designers to understand users on several different levels. For example, customers of an online music store can be modelled in these ways:

- as individual users, profiling characteristics like musical taste, spending habits, level of web literacy, speed of network connection, software used
- as 'actors', profiling the different roles which users take in visiting a site, e.g. browsing, researching, shopping
- in the context of activity moving beyond static profiles to model, for example, the act of finding an album title based on a fragment of a song heard on the radio, previewing other music by the artist and making a purchase
- in the context of communication for e-commerce sites offering the added value of community, whether in terms of direct communication (like bulletin boards) or in terms of 'social navigation' (like Amazon's book referrals).

The Cluetrain Manifesto argues that markets are conversations, made of human beings, not just demographic sectors (Levine, Locke, Searls and Weinberger, 2000). By employing use-case modelling, designers can move beyond statistical representations of customers and profile real, flesh-and-blood, likely site users. They can understand the different roles they play and what they do while online, and begin to facilitate the conversations customers wish to have with the company and each other.

Information architecture

The second discipline that is crucial at the planning stage of an e-commerce site is information architecture. Long before content and functional elements are developed, companies need to examine the use-case models to determine what kinds of content and functionality are needed and how the site is to be structured. Information architecture includes such things as designing labelling systems, determining the level of specificity (granularity) of chunks of information and creating links between units of content. The architecture of a site is critical, for a number of reasons:

1. Without a carefully designed architecture, a website is neither flexible nor scalable. If an e-commerce website can't evolve or grow, neither can the e-commerce business.
2. Without a carefully designed architecture, a website is not maintainable. Major e-commerce websites can contain over 20,000 pages, but even 200 pages are enough to make maintaining a site with poor architecture impossible.
3. Without a carefully designed architecture, a website is neither searchable nor browseable. Searching and browsing are the dominant activities of web users and a customer can only buy what he or she can actually find. More importantly, searching is the primary tool of internet agents (i.e. 'smart' applications trawling the web for prices, product descriptions etc.). These agents are widely held to be the future of internet consumerism.
4. Without a carefully designed architecture, a website is not consistent. Consistency and continuity are prerequisites for customer retention (users go on good faith that if they bookmark a page, it will be there when they comeback). Good architecture is also necessary for successful navigation (imagine the plight of all those poor seventeenth-century sailors if the order of the stars was perpetually 'under renovation'), and for transactions and community building.

Information architecture is approached again in more detail in Chapter 5, Navigation Interfaces. The interested reader is strongly advised to consult *Information Architecture for the World Wide Web* (Rosenfeld and Morville, 1998).

Prototyping and implementation

Moving beyond the planning stages (information gathering and strategy), design teams start 'doing'. The stages that Fleming calls prototyping and implementation are what the average person might normally associate with the design and development of a web site. There are a number of key disciplines involved, including:

- content creators (writers)
- content managers (editors)
- graphic designers and information designers (who will implement the information architecture page by page)
- programmers and administrators (who will build the functionality of the user interface, as well as the back office systems which support the site)
- user experience evaluators (who will test each prototyped design and each piece of content and functionality).

Later in this chapter, the importance of content is discussed further. It is important to note here, however, that much of the value created in a commercial web environment is built from verbal information. Companies must invest in talented writers and editors who understand how to use language online. Furthermore, graphic designers need to understand that web design is not print design. They must be able to produce images appropriate to the medium. Programmers and administrators should not be left to mop-up after the 'design team' is finished. Functionality is content. Non-programmatic content providers and programmers need to work hand in hand.

Finally, evaluation is the key to success in the 'doing' phase. Rigorous field testing will help teams identify and discard inferior content, designs and functions, and to refine those that are well received. By testing early and often, companies avoid lost time and money and are able to sound the alarm before a flawed strategy is put in place.

Launch, maintenance and growth

The final phases of Fleming's cycle — launch, maintenance and growth — will involve all of the disciplines listed. Websites should be treated as organisms that are constantly changing. Content will need to be added, pruned and kept up-to-date. Functionality will need to be debugged and refined. Most importantly, for companies truly interested in creating value, the constant conversation logged by user registrations and user activity will, over time, lead to changing the shape of the site and the site's strategy.

The Importance of Content

While the rest of this book focuses on the arrangement and presentation of content (including functionality), it is important to say a few words about content itself. 'Content is king' has achieved proverbial status, but what does it mean? For e-commerce, it means that content — data — is the primary material from which value is created. Rayport and Sviokla (1999) argue that all contemporary businesses compete in two arenas: a *marketplace* based on physical resources and a *marketspace* based on information. For a long time now, they suggest, the business world has recognised the importance of information, but not its full potential. In general, companies have used information to support the physical value chain of the marketplace. They contend that companies must also view information as a source of value in and of itself, and create value in new ways in the marketspace. This 'virtual value chain' consists of five value-adding steps:

- gathering information
- organising information
- selecting information
- synthesising information
- distributing information.

The concept of the virtual value chain — gathering, manipulating and delivering information in value-added ways — is central to the definition of e-commerce used in this book. The rest of this chapter looks at ways in which content can be used in customer-friendly, value-added ways.

At a minimum, content must help to bridge the 'sensory deprivation gap' of the web. Customers in an online retail environment can't smell, taste or feel, and their vision and hearing are completely limited to the sights and sounds chosen by the designer. This puts a lot of burden on content. A product photo just won't cut it. Too much real world experience has guaranteed that customers ignore stock marketing images. To transform shoppers into buyers, you need words — rich, descriptive, accurate, useful words.

Figure 1.1: http://www.flowersusa.com (May 2000)

Figure 1.1 shows a product page at Flowers USA. The page contains a photo of the product, a marketing blurb ('Shades of orange and pink are brought to life …'), a 'Style' label indicating that the product is 'One-Sided' and a choice of three 'Sizes', namely 'Regular', 'Deluxe' and 'Premium'. This collection of data fails to meet the basic information requirements of the customer.

The first missing piece of information is size. Since the photo is a cut-out against white rather a picture of the product alongside other objects, the customer has no sense of scale. Scanning the page, the customer wondering about size will probably latch on to 'Sizes Available', but the information there is not too helpful. 'Regular', 'Deluxe' and 'Premium' are meaningless labels — it can be assumed that each one is bigger than the last, since each one is $10 more, but that's all. Realistically, customers have a good idea of the size of a carnation blossom, but since they are paying a premium on the vase, it is important to state whether it is 10 cm or 30 cm tall. For that matter, the customer does not even know whether the vase is made of glass or plastic.

Beyond size, the composition of the bouquet is ill-defined. Both the photo and the blurb tell the customer that there are roses and carnations, but not (even roughly) how many of each. A price of

$60 for six roses and two accent carnations is a good deal, but not the other way around. Perhaps it is the composition, and not the size, that 'Deluxe' and 'Premium' refer to. The customer is left guessing.

It is the ambiguity of the labels that does the most damage. The 'Style' label is particularly irritating. In all likelihood, 'Style' is an attribute label straight out of the database, useful to the stockroom but not to customers. And what does 'One-Sided' mean? That the product must be displayed against a wall and only viewed from one side?

In summary, on this page the customer is left with:

- a photo and a blurb that can't be completely trusted and neither of which actually says exactly what the customer is buying
- 'style' information that is perplexing
- a choice of three size/price categories with no information to distinguish between them.

There are two buttons below the product: 'Back' and 'Order.' Which is the most likely to be chosen? Far from creating value through information, this page fails to meet the most basic of needs — telling customers what they are buying.

Figure 1.2: http://www.flowersusa.com (March 2000)

Meeting the most basic of needs is a start, but a customer-friendly site design goes well beyond that. To truly use information in a value-added way, customers should understand not just what they are buying, but *why*. Figure 1.2 shows another page from Flowers USA, this time the 'Anniversary' section chosen from the 'Occasions' menu.

To move from 'what' to 'why', vendors need to create context. Allowing the customers the opportunity to browse 'By Occasion' is a nice filtering service (part of the virtual value chain), but the site does not capitalise on the chance to create value by providing *information about the occasion*. If customers are visiting this page, they are engaged in two activities — they are shopping for flowers and (on a higher level) they are planning a romantic event. Information can and should be used to support both activities. For example, a chart showing the traditional anniversary gifts might reinforce the decision to buy flowers (flowers are the traditional fourth year gift) or help customers choose the most appropriate arrangement (such as the 'golden candle' centrepiece for the golden anniversary). Likewise, the act of event planning can be supported with ideas for romantic meals, locations and activities.

Surprisingly, some of the best examples of contextual value creation come from online grocery stores. It's true that the online grocer is a business model fraught with monumental logistical challenges. But whether or not these challenges are met, they have a good deal to teach the e-commerce industry about repackaging a business in an infocentric way.

Groceryworks (Figure 1.3) uses information to create contextual value in a number of ways. First, it provides two information management utilities for the customer, both the standard shopping cart and a shopping list. This allows the customers to create their own context by organising their own needs. Second, Groceryworks offers recipes, sometimes from celebrity chefs. This information is a free gift to the customers, who can print it out and use it whether or not they buy the ingredients online. It creates value, and thus goodwill, and thus return visitors. Combined with convenient links to the ingredients listed, it also creates buyers. Third, the grocer realises that most people eat to live, not the other way around. If customers are doing their grocery shopping online, they're probably trying to save time to use for other things, like being with family. And so the site publishes recommendations for family activities, which is a sign that the company knows its customers — and cares. Finally, it provides articles (again by experts) on nutrition and health. With every line, the company is creating more value, more goodwill and a richer context to help customers understand why they should buy that particular can of beans.

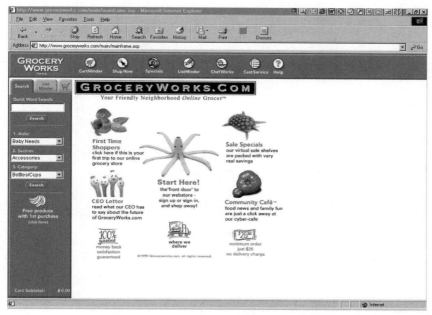

Figure 1.3: http://www.groceryworks.com (February 2000)

Another e-grocer, Peapod (Figure 1.4), takes a slightly different and even more 'down home' approach. Rather than gourmet recipes, it offers guidelines for the well stocked pantry and recommendations for making school lunches. This particular site also offers a pseudo-personalised 'grocery portal', giving the customer the opportunity to build the grocery store of his or her choosing.

Businesses whose products are easily digitised, such as book and music vendors, need to take advantage of the opportunity to provide very thick context, including samples. Music retailer CD Quest (Figure 1.5) uses the information carrying capacity of the web to add value in two ways. First, it delivers the services of a music magazine as well as a music store by providing in-depth artist profiles and interviews, industry news, etc. Second, like many online music merchants, it takes advantage of the fact that its product is information (digitised sound). This means that it can offer made-to-order CDs.

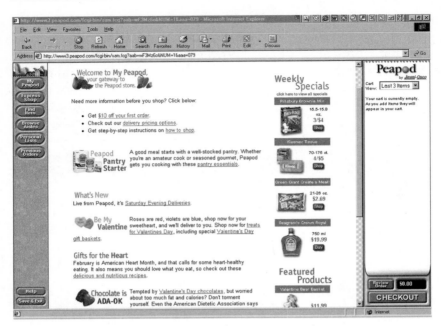

Figure 1.4: http://www.peapod.com (February 2000)

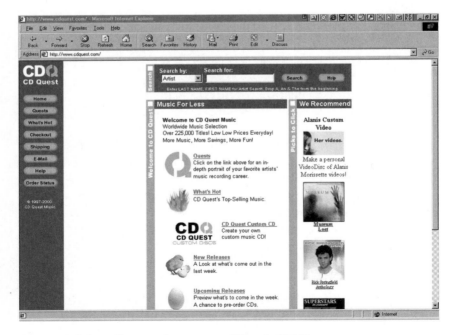

Figure 1.5: http://www.cdquest.com (March 2000)

While CD Quest uses the digital nature of recorded music to offer a new product, Barnes and Noble Music uses it to display an existing product in a value-added way. B&N Music offers an excellent service called the 'listening wall' (Figure 1.6) which allows customers to sample a wide range of music directly over the web. The listening wall facilitates 'audio browsing' and encourages exploratory purchases.

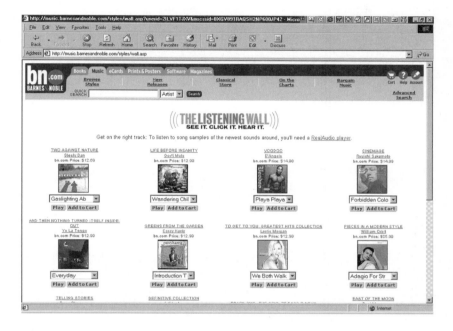

Figure 1.6: http://music.barnesandnoble.com (March 2000)

The same service is built into individual product pages, adding value to the process of planned purchase decision-making (Figure 1.7).

The publishing industry, not surprisingly, has also demonstrated an understanding of the value and use of information. Book retailers have added value in a number of ways:

- by contextualising product offerings with excellent search engines
- with internal and external content like author biographies, interviews, news and reviews
- with reader generated content.

Figure 1.7: http://music.barnesandnoble.com (March 2000)

Most impressive, however, are the efforts of book publishers who make use of their legal ownership of the content of the books to create highly intensive information environments. For example, the technology press O'Reilly provides computer industry news, software and programming tutorials, product reviews and editorial content. In this way it creates a site that can be consumed as a publication in its own right. Consequently, the O'Reilly brand (trustworthy information for professional technologists) is constantly reinforced, and the purchase decision is driven, not by hype, but by tangibly demonstrating the overwhelming quality of the O'Reilly product (Figure 1.8).

Furthermore, O'Reilly allows readers to 'virtually' thumb through a book by reading sample chapters and viewing the table of contents and the index (Figure 1.9), thus overcoming one of the great limitations of online book buying.

Finally, information can be used to support decision-making very effectively through 'just-in-time' delivery. For example, purchasing a computer can be a daunting task for customers and so computer manufacturers/resellers must provide a great deal of timely, relevant information to facilitate the process. When purchasing a computer from either Dell or Gateway, it is possible for the customer to select upgrades and downgrades, thus

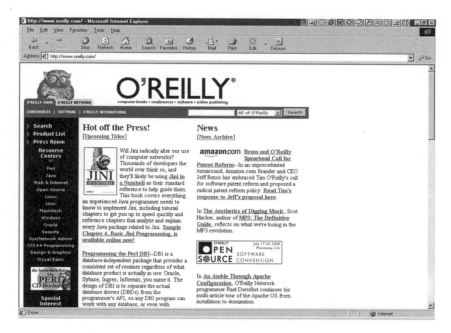

Figure 1.8: http://www.oreilly.com (March 2000)

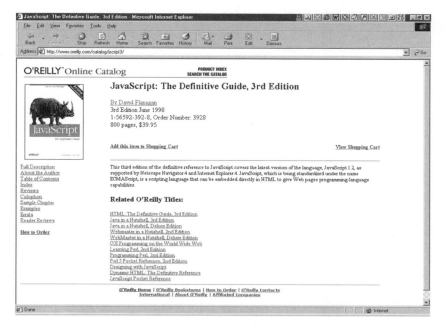

Figure 1.9: http://www.oreilly.com (March 2000)

customising the system. This is a tremendously valuable feature and an important part of the brand of both companies. But the process can be agonising when a customer is asked to choose between a 40 GB Ultra ATA hard drive and an 18 GB SCSI Ultra2/wide hard drive, or between the Microsoft Internet Keyboard and the QuietKey Keyboard. Both sites provide a 'tell me more' feature but there is a big difference in the quality of the two services.

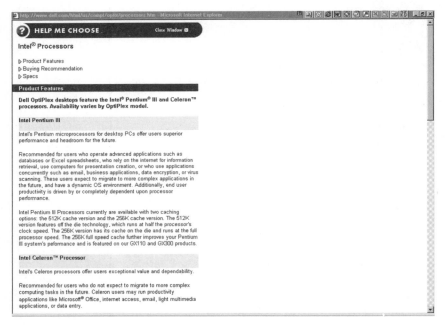

Figure 1.10: http://www.dell.com (February 2000)

Dell's 'Help Me Choose' feature (Figure 1.10), which opens in a new window, provides users with:

- a summary of features
- a comparison table of specifications
- recommendations for purchase based on planned activity
- a glossary.

Most importantly, the help files are very comprehensive, providing information on almost every option which was presented to the user on the previous page.

Gateway (Figure 1.11) provides a similar feature, but less effectively. Because it does not open in a separate window, customers who read a few component descriptions must do a good deal of back-button clicking to return to the form. Also, the feature does not include tabular data, the natural arrangement for comparing several similar products. Rather, Gateway requires that customers follow a separate link for each item. Since there is no glossary, the 'help' file is often as opaque as the product name. Finally, the feature is not comprehensive and provides no support for migraine-inducing decisions like choosing a processor or memory configuration.

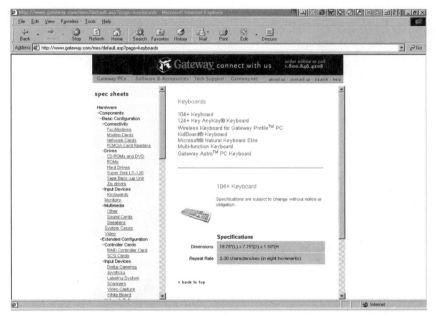

Figure 1.11: http://www.gateway.com (February 2000)

Conventional wisdom says that the e-commerce model is only suitable for 'information intensive' businesses. Conventional wisdom is right, but leaves out one important detail. *All* businesses are information intensive, or at least they *can* be. Becoming information intensive means utilising the power of the internet as a communications medium to provide rich descriptive and contextual content which will facilitate the decision-making and purchasing processes, improve branding and customer relationships and add value to the online shopping experience.

CHAPTER 2:

Designing for Speed

Why Speed is Important

Like any computer network, the internet is only as fast as its slowest link. The backbones of the internet, which interconnect the thousands of smaller organisational networks and internet service providers (ISPs), are technological marvels — high bandwidth, high speed and highly reliable. They're also highly irrelevant. For the home user, all that really matters is the low bandwidth, low speed and the sometimes unreliable internet connection provided by a modem and (in most cases) a standard twisted-wire phone line. Yet, companies continue to build bulky, slow loading websites — and then pat themselves on the back for it. As Bob Tedeschi (1999b) commented, companies that are 'constantly adjusting to operating at lightning speeds to keep pace with internet technologies, must reconcile themselves to the fact that their customers are living in what amounts to slow motion on the other end of the line. As a result, these businesses have to make difficult decisions about how to attract and keep customers within the limited bandwidth available.'

Speed is important because customers see e-commerce as a time-saving device. When e-commerce sites fail to deliver, customers have one less reason to choose online shopping. This chapter is dedicated to the idea that it's simply bad business to make customers wait. But just how bad? Zona Research suggests that unacceptable download times could cost the e-commerce industry in the US alone $4.35 billion each year (Zona Research, 1999).

Figure 2.1 shows the US West homepage. There is nothing extraordinary about it; visually, it's actually quite simple. And yet loading this 'simple' page required my browser to send over twenty separate requests to the server to download over 100 KB worth of images. This was a questionable effort since most of the images, as you can see, are just pictures of text. The loading time was further lengthened by the fact that the document consists almost entirely of JavaScript scripts, forms, tables and image maps, all of which require extensive client-side processing.

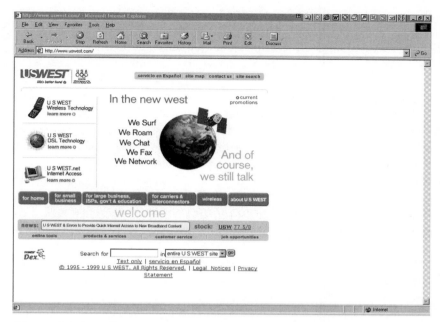

Figure 2.1: http://www.uswest.com (February 2000)

Figure 2.2: http://www.uswest.com. After 10 seconds (February 2000)

I visited US West from home at several different times of day over the course of a week. I used an established ISP and, like over more than half of all home-users (Upsdell, 2000), I used a 33.6 Kbps modem. The homepage took an average of 50 seconds to load. Figure 2.2 shows what the average user might see after 10 seconds of patiently waiting:

To its credit, US West does provide a link to a text-only version of the site, which will provide faster service to those who desire it. However, the link is at the bottom of the page and users with lower screen resolutions (see Chapter 3) will not even be aware of it unless they scroll down the page. Furthermore, 'text only' is an all-or-nothing proposition. Why force the customer to choose between barren text and an interminable wait? Instead, why not strive for an aesthetic, functional site which is optimised for speed?

The truth is, neither e-commerce companies nor customers can do very much about delays and traffic jams 'out there' on the network. But what customers can do is:

- buy faster machines or subscribe to faster connection services (a financial burden)
- schedule their time online to avoid peak times (an inconvenience)
- take their online business to a faster site.

Since customers seem most willing to exercise this last option, e-commerce designers need to do whatever they can to increase the performance of their websites. There are two ways in which this can be accomplished:

- optimising back-end applications (the web server, the database management system, e-commerce applications, CGI programs, etc.
- optimising the content of the site.

The focus of this chapter is on techniques for optimising content. (The optimisation of back-end applications is primarily an administrative issue and back-end tuning is very product specific. Interested readers should therefore look for resources which offer a tight focus on optimising performance for a particular piece of software.)

In general, the content of a web page consists of four things: text, HTML, embedded media and embedded programs, all of which can be optimised for speed.

Guidelines for Optimising Text

Strunk and White (1979) argue that 'vigorous writing is concise. A sentence should contain no unnecessary words, a paragraph no unnecessary sentences, for the same reason that a drawing should have no unnecessary lines and a machine no unnecessary parts.' Pulling it forward thirty years, Byte.com editor Paul Schindler (quoted in Smith, 2000) says that good web copy comes from 'writing like Ernest Hemingway. Blowing the wind out of the reader.' Text is arguably the most important, information-rich content that a site can provide for users, but unless it is packaged well, its value is lost.

Jakob Nielsen (1997a) provides a framework for applying these bits of advice to the web when he calls for designers to create more scannable text. Some techniques for making text scannable include:

- organising information in order of importance
- focusing the user's attention through highlighted words, lists and meaningful titles and subtitles
- creating atomic (single idea) paragraphs
- reducing the word count.

Derrick Story (2000) also offers a handful of suggestions for writing better web copy, including:

- writing to address user interests
- using an appropriate tone and the active voice
- editing, not just writing
- avoiding grammatical and spelling errors
- using a site-wide style guide
- putting more effort into pre-writing planning
- taking advantage of hypertextuality (in moderation).

Notice that only Neilsen's suggestion of word count reduction will make the page *load* faster. The rest of the advice improves the speed with which the customer can *consume* the information. If information is prioritised, users won't need to wait for the full page to load to get to the meat of the content. The use of lists, for example, will allow users to run through content more quickly to find the information which is of interest, while the atomicity of paragraphs ensures that sections can be skipped safely. Both online and offline, the job of the writer is to organise information, act as interpreter and, most of all, get the message out (Dougherty, 1997).

Figure 2.3 shows a product page from Macys.com, which does a nice job of presenting the customer with an easily digested chunk of information. The bulleted points are scannable, and although the copy is a little advertising-like, it is well directed. Words like 'classic', 'cotton' and 'imported' are all phrases which a Macy's customer is likely to be looking for.

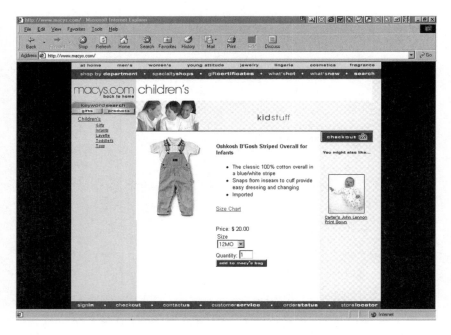

Figure 2.3: http://www.macys.com (March 2000)

Unfortunately, the Macy's 'Size Chart' (Figure 2.4) is anything but easily digestible and does not even render fully on the screen. Meanwhile, Walmart (Figure 2.5), which does not have an easily consumed product description, does have a very easy-to-use size guide, which is specific to the product shown and does not involve hunting for information.

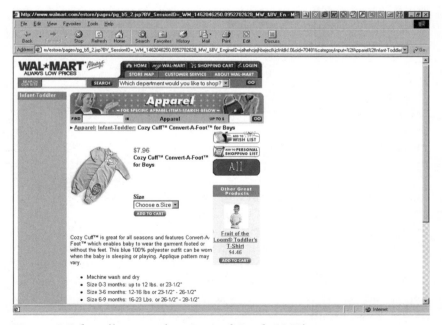

Size Chart - OshKosh B'gosh					Size Chart - OshKosh B'gosh					Size Chart - OshKosh B'gosh			
AGE	SIZE	HEIGHT	WEIGHT		AGE	SIZE	HEIGHT	WEIGHT		AGE	SIZE	HEIGHT	WEI
Newborns	3/6 Months	66cm/26in	7kg/15lbs		Newborns	3/6 Months	66cm/26in	7kg/15lbs		Newborns	3/6 Months	66cm/26in	7kg/
	6/9 Months	71cm/28in	8kg/18lbs			6/9 Months	71cm/28in	8kg/18lbs			6/9 Months	71cm/28in	8kg/
Infants	12 Months	76cm/30in	9kg/20lbs		Infants	12 Months	76cm/30in	9kg/20lbs		Infants	12 Months	76cm/30in	9kg/
	18 Months	81cm/32in	11kg/24lbs			18 Months	81cm/32in	11kg/24lbs			18 Months	81cm/32in	11kg/
	24 Months*	86cm/34in	13kg/29lbs			24 Months*	86cm/34in	13kg/29lbs			24 Months*	86cm/34in	13kg/
Toddlers	2*	86cm/34in	13kg/29lbs		Toddlers	2*	86cm/34in	13kg/29lbs		Toddlers	2*	86cm/34in	13kg/
	3	94cm/37in	15kg/33lbs			3	94cm/37in	15kg/33lbs			3	94cm/37in	15kg/
	4	102cm/40in	17kg/37lbs			4	102cm/40in	17kg/37lbs			4	102cm/40in	17kg/
Girls/Boys	4	105cm/41in	17kg/37lbs		Girls/Boys	4	105cm/41in	17kg/37lbs		Girls/Boys	4	105cm/41in	17kg/
	5	109cm/43in	20kg/44lbs			5	109cm/43in	20kg/44lbs			5	109cm/43in	20kg/
	6	117cm/46in	22kg/48lbs			6	117cm/46in	22kg/48lbs			6	117cm/46in	22kg/
	6X	122cm/48in	27kg/53lbs			6X	122cm/48in	27kg/53lbs			6X	122cm/48in	27kg/

* Sizes 24 Months and 2 Year are the same. The 24 Month have a snap-up crotch for easier diaper changing, while the 2 Year does not

* Sizes 24 Months and 2 Year are the same. The 24 Month have a snap-up crotch for easier diaper changing, while the 2 Year does not

* Sizes 24 Months and 2 Year are the same. The 24 Month has a snap-up crotch for easier diaper changing, while the 2 Year d

Size Chart - OshKosh B'gosh					Size Chart - OshKosh B'gosh					Size Chart - OshKosh B'gosh			
AGE	SIZE	HEIGHT	WEIGHT		AGE	SIZE	HEIGHT	WEIGHT		AGE	SIZE	HEIGHT	WEI
Newborns	3/6 Months	66cm/26in	7kg/15lbs		Newborns	3/6 Months	66cm/26in	7kg/15lbs		Newborns	3/6 Months	66cm/26in	7kg/
	6/9 Months	71cm/28in	8kg/18lbs			6/9 Months	71cm/28in	8kg/18lbs			6/9 Months	71cm/28in	8kg/
Infants	12 Months	76cm/30in	9kg/20lbs		Infants	12 Months	76cm/30in	9kg/20lbs		Infants	12 Months	76cm/30in	9kg/
	18 Months	81cm/32in	11kg/24lbs			18 Months	81cm/32in	11kg/24lbs			18 Months	81cm/32in	11kg/
	24 Months*	86cm/34in	13kg/29lbs			24 Months*	86cm/34in	13kg/29lbs			24 Months*	86cm/34in	13kg/
Toddlers	2*	86cm/34in	13kg/29lbs		Toddlers	2*	86cm/34in	13kg/29lbs		Toddlers	2*	86cm/34in	13kg/
	3	94cm/37in	15kg/33lbs			3	94cm/37in	15kg/33lbs			3	94cm/37in	15kg/
	4	102cm/40in	17kg/37lbs			4	102cm/40in	17kg/37lbs			4	102cm/40in	17kg/
Girls/Boys	4	105cm/41in	17kg/37lbs		Girls/Boys	4	105cm/41in	17kg/37lbs		Girls/Boys	4	105cm/41in	17kg/
	5	109cm/43in	20kg/44lbs			5	109cm/43in	20kg/44lbs			5	109cm/43in	20kg/
	6	117cm/46in	22kg/48lbs			6	117cm/46in	22kg/48lbs			6	117cm/46in	22kg/
	6X	122cm/48in	27kg/53lbs			6X	122cm/48in	27kg/53lbs			6X	122cm/48in	27kg/

Figure 2.4: http://www.macys.com (March 2000)

Cozy Cuff™ Convert-A-Foot™ for Boys

$7.96

Cozy Cuff™ is great for all seasons and features Convert-A-Foot™ which enables baby to wear the garment footed or without the feet. This blue 100% polyester outfit can be worn when the baby is sleeping or playing. Applique pattern may vary.

- Machine wash and dry
- Size 0-3 months: up to 12 lbs. or 23-1/2"
- Size 3-6 months: 12-16 lbs or 23-1/2" - 26-1/2"
- Size 6-9 months: 16-23 Lbs. or 26-1/2" - 28-1/2"

Fruit of the Loom® Toddler's T-Shirt $4.46

Figure 2.5: http://www.walmart.com (March 2000)

In the previous chapter, I discussed the use of information to create value. An important part of creating that value is delivering the content in a manner suited to the medium. While there is only one way to optimise text for download speed (use less), there are many ways to optimise it for speed of consumption. Making it easy for a customer to sift through information quickly is an important part of customer-friendly design.

Guidelines for Optimising HTML

HTML tags are also just text, but even text can add up to dozens of KB of data. Customers don't see HTML tags, they see content. In order to make as much time as possible available for downloading real content, designers must minimise the amount of HTML which a customer must download to render that content.

The first thing a designer can do is work to avoid repeating tags. Using redundant tags can quickly double the physical size of a page. I performed a simple experiment: I wrote two pages, each with a bulleted list containing fifteen identical links. On one page, the entire list was inside a <font></font> container which set the colour of the text. On the other page each list item was inside its own font container. The pages rendered in an identical fashion, but the page with redundant tags was nearly 500 bytes larger. That's not much of a difference, but imagine the designer of a page with 150 links making the same error; the user now has to download 5 KB of tags that do exactly nothing. The <font> lesson applies to <style> tags as well. Whenever possible, designers should build page-level style sheets, rather than repeat inline <style> tags. Even better, use external style sheets to share between pages, which will be saved in the local cache and promote a consistent look-and-feel to boot. (See Mulder 1998a for further examples.)

Similarly, designers need to avoid restating default values. Redundancy does not always mean repetition; it can also mean restating global values. If the <body> tag of a document defines the text colour, <font> and <style> tags should only be used to identify exceptions, not reinforce the rules. Likewise, designers need to be aware of the HTML-defined default values of tag attributes. For example, the default alignment for a new paragraph is left, so although <p align='left'> is 500% larger than <p>, the extra bytes don't create extra functionality. (See Mulder 1998a for further examples.)

Redundancy can also be reduced by using *root-relative* and

directory-relative URLs, rather than *absolute* URLs. An absolute URL includes all domain and path information, such as 'http://www.somewebsite.com/products/sports/frisbees.html'. A root-relative URL takes advantage of the defaults built into HTML, namely, that unless stated otherwise, the domain remains the same. For example, '/products/sports/frisbees.html' is identical in function to the absolute URL above. The leading '/' indicates that the path name starts at the root directory. Finally, a directory-relative URL starts the search for the target file in the folder where the link is located. Thus the 'frisbees' page could link to the 'footballs' page in the same directory by simply linking to 'footballs.html.' If the designers of 'somewebsite.com' put together an index page with links to 100 products, relative and root URLs could do away with up to 2.5 KB of redundant HTML.

In writing HTML with speed in mind, designers need to be cautious when using 'what you see is what you get' HTML generators. Generators make building web pages easier, but they make redundancy control more difficult. The reason is simple: redundant HTML tags need to be written. If a designer is hand coding a page, the 298 redundant tags in my bulleted list example (149 <font> open tags and 149 </font> close tags) would be a time consuming, tedious task. For a human being, it's easier to solve the problem creatively than to type (or even drag-and-drop) all those tags. Unfortunately, tediousness doesn't faze computer applications, which often find it easier to repeat a task 150 times than to think it through. Furthermore, generators often have very poor garbage collection functionality. For example, if I want to make a word red, I can write:

<font color='red'>Word</font>.

If I change my mind and want it to be blue, I can change the HTML to:

<font color='blue'>Word</font>.

However, changing your mind while working with a generator can lead to extraneous code, like:

<font color='red'><font color='blue'>Word</font></font>

or

<font color='red'></font><font color='blue'>Word</font>.

Designers using generators must schedule development time to edit the work of their well meaning but ultimately stupid digital assistants. More than once, I've been able to reduce a page created by a generator to one third the size without sacrificing appearance or functionality.

A final form of redundancy comes from repeating file names. Even in relative URLs, names are often repeated. To minimise the impact of the repetition, designers should choose a consistent and terse naming convention for all files and directories. Remember that file and directory names are for the convenience of the developer, not the customer. The customer doesn't care if the link points to 'products/sport_equipment_and_clothing/frisbees.html' or to 'prod/sport/fris.html'. Designers should take the space saved by shorter file names and use it to build better *link labels*; customers do care whether a link is labelled 'Sport' or 'Sport Equipment and Clothing'. Likewise, the names of media files (images, etc.) should be kept short and should be stored in a common, high level directory (facilitating root-relative linking). (See Mulder 1998a for further examples.)

So much for redundancy. The second way to speed up HTML is to use complex objects, like tables, wisely. Web browsers read pages line by line. That means that when a browser encounters a complex object, nothing happens until the entire object is parsed and rendered. If the entire page is set as a table, well, you do the math.

There are several things that a designer can do to improve the use of tables in a page:

- don't use them (or elements of them) unless necessary. Often other tags can accomplish the same effect as a table in a way that is simpler for the browser to render. For example, designers should make use of image alignment tags to 'wrap' text around a graphic or photo. Likewise, inserting extra rows and columns into a table to create white space is inefficient. The 'cellpadding' and 'cellspacing' attributes can be used to create a similar product

- chop tables up into several smaller tables. In reality, a page containing three small tables does not reach completion any faster than the same page organised as one large table. However, with the small tables, the page loads incrementally so the user has access to the contents of each table as soon as that table has been fully read. In contrast, big tables load in an all-or-nothing fashion

- never nest tables. HTML provides two attributes, 'rowspan' and 'colspan', which allow for the creation of complex tables without nesting.

You should refer to Mulder (1998b) for further examples.

The third way to optimise HTML is to create separate development and production files. Comments are an extremely important ingredient in creating high quality, easy-to-maintain code, even if that code is just HTML. However, there is no reason to make a customer download all of the comments that were written for the benefit of the developer. Editing out comments before putting an HTML file in the production folder can shave off valuable bytes (and therefore seconds). Likewise, Mulder (1998a) points out that line breaks and strings of white space are generally ignored by browsers. The following chunk of HTML is optimised for the ease of use of the developer:

```
<ul>
<li>
       Item One
</li>
<li>
       Item Two
</li>
<li>
       Item Three
</li>
<li>
       Item Four
</li>
<li>
       Item Five
</li>
</ul>
```

However, it can be rewritten to the production file as:

```
<ul><li>Item One</li>
<li>Item Two</li>
<li>Item Three</li>
<li>Item Four</li>
<li>Item Five</li></ul>
```

The rendered page is identical, but the HTML is about 33% smaller.

Before moving on, one note of caution is needed. HTML

optimisation is about efficiency, *not* evisceration. The job of the designer is to get rid of unnecessary HTML while still writing robust HTML. Try not to go overboard. For example, don't be tempted to save space by not closing tags that should be closed, just because some browsers will let you get away with it. Likewise, don't get rid of truly useful attributes, like 'alt', 'width' and 'height' for images (see below).

Guidelines for Optimising Embedded Media

The damage that can be done by sloppy HTML is mitigated by the fact that text is very lightweight. This is not true of the image files which are embedded in pages. Above we saw that 298 unnecessary <font> tags only added up to 5 KB. A *single* unnecessary image, video or sound file can weigh in at anywhere from 10 KB to 1 MB. Although the guidelines in this section are applicable to all media files, I focus on images because they afford the most opportunity for tweaking.

Anyone who has been online long enough to remember what life was like before the graphical web came along will fight tooth and nail to keep us from going back to the barren world of pure TEXT. But to build fast loading, customer-friendly websites, designers must be ruthlessly discriminating about what media files they use. The constant design question should be: does the value added by the embedded object outweigh the cost of including it? Sometimes the answer is 'yes', for example a company logo, a picture of a product or a map with directions to a physical store. More often the answer is 'no' as with that animated e-mail icon, or flashing 'NEW!' image. A picture is worth a thousand words, but on the web, a mid-sized picture costs as much to deliver as *four* thousand words, so what has been gained? When you do include graphics, follow the guidelines below. Further examples of these techniques in practice can be found in Cook (1998).

Guideline I

First, give the browser information about the image. No image should ever be placed on the web without specifying its 'width' and 'height'. If the browser knows how large an image will be, it can set aside the space and go on loading the page. Otherwise it needs to wait until the image has fully loaded before it continues to read/render.

Guideline 2

Second, when it is beneficial, use text, HTML and/or style sheets to simulate images.

Sometimes, a word is a design product in and of itself. Take a look at Figure 2.6 (I won't even mention how long this one took to load!).

Figure 2.6: http://www.cocacola.com (February 2000)

The signature look of the Coca-Cola trademark is a major asset for the company — on the web or anywhere else. I would argue that maintaining control over the look of the words 'Coca-Cola' is a requirement for maintaining brand. Just the same, what did US West gain from exerting absolute control over the look of words like 'For Home' and 'For Small Businesses' (see Figure 2.1)? Designers should be cautious of using pictures of words where the words themselves would do. This doesn't mean that words need to be presented as plain text. Using style sheets and/or HTML, designers can put together interesting graphical elements in a leaner fashion than embedding files. See Figure 2.7 for an example. The top 'Home' button is an image, the middle one is text with <font> tags in a table cell, and the bottom one was created with a style sheet.

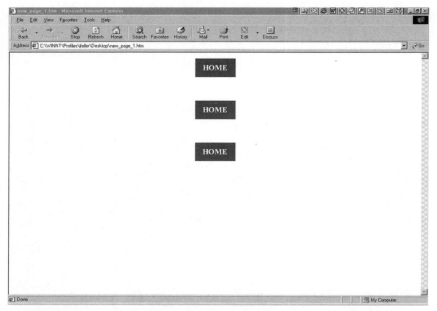

Figure 2.7: From top to bottom: an image, HTML tags and style sheet

It's true that the only way for the designer to have *absolute* control over the font attributes is to use the image. But designers must ask themselves just how important is it to have the word 'home' in Helvetica rather than Arial or some other san-serif font? Does the value gained make up for the fact that the image is fifty times larger than the corresponding HTML and style sheet arrangements?

Notice that at the beginning of the discussion of this guideline I advised designers to use this technique 'when it is beneficial'. Sometimes the style sheet, table etc. is actually slower. For example, on subsequent pages, the HTML is downloaded anew, but the image is cached. Designers should always test a variety of methods and choose the most appropriate for the situation.

Guideline 3

Third, use HTML and/or CSS to augment images. If an image has a large area of a single colour, it should be trimmed down to take advantage of the layout and colour capabilities of HTML. Figure 2.8 shows two images. The one on the left is 300 x 300 pixels and should never appear on a web page. Instead, the image on the right, which is 72 x 72 pixels, should be placed in a 300 x 300 pixel table cell with a black background.

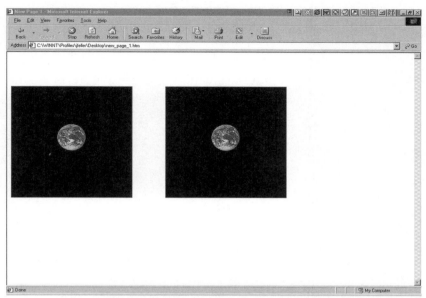

Figure 2.8: A 300 x 300 pixel image (8 KB) vs a 72 x 72 pixel image in 300 x 300 pixel table cell (5 KB)

Guideline 4

Avoid animated images. Animated image files use the same technology as a flip-book cartoon. The image actually contains dozens of similar images which are cycled through to create the animated effect. This means that a tiny image is actually made up of 10–20 images, just as large. Figure 2.9 shows a handful of animated e-mail icons, all rather small, but weighing in at an average of 7.5 KB.

Guideline 5

Reuse images. If you use an image, use it throughout the site. The first time an image is viewed, the browser issues an HTTP request for the file and waits for the server to deliver. As I mentioned above, after that the image is in the browser's cache and can be read locally. Thus, a large graphical navigation bar takes forever to load on the home page but seems instantaneous on subsequent pages. Designers must learn to take advantage of the browser cache to maximise the use a site gets out of an image. Images with shared features can also be partially recycled, as illustrated below. Figure 2.10 shows two title banners with a lot in common. By breaking the two images into three (Figure 2.11) and reconstituting them in a table, the designer is able to recycle part of the image and improve the performance of the site.

Figure 2.9: Animated e-mail icons, ranging from 2–20 KB in size

Figure 2.10: Two distinct title banners

Figure 2.11: Recyclable building blocks

The images in Figure 2.10 require transferring 26 KB from the server; the images in Figure 2.11 only require transferring 17 KB. The savings could be further increased by recycling even more of the image. Better yet (unless you absolutely must have 'Products' and 'Services' written in the 'Viner Hand ITC' font), replace the right half of the image with an HTML/style sheet 'cheat', as above. Animated images can also be made smaller by modifying the 'flip-book' so that only the parts of the image that move are actually repeated.

Guideline 6
Choose and use image formats appropriately. The majority of images on the web are JPG and GIF files. As a general rule of thumb:

- GIFs are better for images with clean lines and large blocks of single colours (like drawings)
- JPGs are optimised for images with more complex colour patterns (like photos).

Again, designers should save potential images in multiple formats to compare quality and size. The different compression formats used can mean tremendous variation in size.

Jennifer Niederst (1999) deals briefly with both GIF and JPG optimisation. Probably the most helpful book on producing and optimising graphics for the web is Lynda Weinman's (1999) *Designing Web Graphics.3*. Weinman's website, Lynda.com (http://www.lynda.com) is also a rich source of advice.

Guidelines for Optimising Embedded Programs
Full-blown programs, like a JAVA applet, should be treated in much the same way as an image. Consider factors such as its necessity, size versus quality, etc. However, further attention needs to be focused on scripting languages such as JavaScript. These languages are just text, but they can slow down page loads considerably because, unlike HTML, they are complete programming languages which must be 'run' by being interpreted by the browser.

As with embedded media files and complex tables, the most effective optimisation technique is to use scripts sparingly. For example, both HTML and JavaScript can open a link in a new window, so unless you need the extra control that comes with JavaScript, use the HTML.

Furthermore, scripts shouldn't be used for 'bells and whistles'. Scrolling marquees and other eye-candy add little in the way of useful functionality. Designers should save the space for scripts that do something useful, such as providing a shopping cart, serving up customised content or providing a more interactive interface. Even something informative, like inserting the time on a web page, should be given careful consideration. (JavaScript creates a new date/time value by checking the user's system clock. Why waste load time to give the user information that is already elsewhere on the screen?)

If a script goes on to a page, it should be well written. There are a dozen ways to make a given programming language perform a particular task and some are much more efficient than others. Designers should take full advantage of the capabilities of the scripting language for creating elegant, reusable functions.

Addressing the need for speed is one of the most important things an e-commerce design team can do to build more customer-friendly sites. Strategists and site architects must make the speed of an e-commerce website a priority at the outset. Top level decision-makers must set realistic standards for multimedia and programmatic content and weigh the 'time factor' of such content against the value added. Written content creators must answer Nielsen's call for scannability, especially if they are coming from a print background. As we saw above, writing for the web is different from writing for print, and both writers and editors must address these differences. Multimedia content creators must optimise images and other files both at the moment of creation and in the delivery of these files to the customer. HTML coders and programmers must strive for both leaner pages and pages which are simpler for the browser to load and render.

CHAPTER 3:

Designing for Flexibility

Why Flexibility is Important

The last chapter argued that it was bad business to keep the customer waiting and so designers must therefore be committed to designing for speed. This chapter looks at another of the fundamental requirements for delivering customer-friendly web content — flexibility. The web works because it is an open platform, allowing different kinds of computer hardware and software (and thus human beings) to share information. Designers need to be committed to reinforcing these open standards, not detracting from them.

There are both short-term and long-term gains associated with this commitment. In the short term, flexible design leads to sites which are useful to and usable by the widest possible audience, or in the case of e-commerce, the widest possible market. In the long term, adhering to flexible design strengthens the overall platform of the web, making it a more powerful medium for the future creation and exchange of value.

The need for flexibility arises out of the nature of the web itself. In print design, our control over the product is limited only by the technology and technique used to produce it. Once a magazine page is printed, it's done. It does not change. In web design, however, our control over the product is further dependent on the technology used to consume it. Even a so-called static web page doesn't exist in a finished form until a browser has downloaded and rendered it for the user. The medium dictates the design strategy. With print, we design for control because we *can*. With the web, we design for flexibility because we *must*. Specifically, designers must strive for two different kinds of flexibility: technological interoperability and user accessibility.

Interoperability

Interoperability is affected by the following:

- hardware
- operating systems
- browsers
- user preference.

If every e-commerce customer were using the same hardware, operating system, application software and application settings, there would be no need for technological interoperability. But, of course, they are not, and so there is.

Hardware

There are a wide variety of devices capable of accessing web content, including touch-screen kiosks, mobile phones, PDAs and hand-held computers, laptop and desktop PCs, high-end workstations and multi-processor servers. These devices all have different capacities for input and output — some have mice and/or keyboards and others don't, some have monitors and/or speakers and others don't, etc. Furthermore, monitors, which are the primary output device for web content, are also subject to extreme variations in screen size, resolution, colour depth and graphics support — all of which can cause pages to render in unexpected ways, or not at all.

Operating systems

As with hardware, operating systems vary greatly. Various versions of Microsoft Windows, Mac OS, IBM's OS/2, different hand-held operating systems and the many flavours of UNIX (like Linux) are all used as web browsing platforms and they all have an impact on the presentation of web pages. For example, the OS determines the level of support for graphical elements and, if they are supported, how they appear to the user. For example, Mac OS, Windows 98 and Linux all size and display HTML form elements differently. More importantly, the OS determines what kind of application software (web browsers and related software) is supported.

Browsers

Browsers from different vendors, and different versions of browsers from the same vendor, vary widely. Some browsers don't support graphics, others do. Some implement and support the HTML standard, others offer non-standard extensions. The interpreters that execute scripting languages like JavaScript often behave slightly differently in different browsers, if they are there at all. And there are a number of technologies (plug-ins, Java, animated GIFs, frames, etc.) which designers often take for granted but which are really options — it can't be assumed that all users will have access to these technologies.

User preference

Finally, designers must take into account variation in user preferences. Users can turn images on and off, disable JavaScript and Java or choose not to install (or else disable) plug-ins. They can make browser windows any size and proportional shape they want and override page defined font sizes and page colours.

Accessibility

The second important type of flexibility is accessibility. E-commerce webs are not glossy brochures — they are places of business and they must be made accessible to all customers. This means that designers must take into account customers with a variety of abilities, including individuals who cannot see or hear, or cannot use a keyboard or a mouse, and so on. While companies are not responsible for developing and distributing the supporting technology that allows, for example, a blind person to read online, they do need to be committed to delivering, either as primary or alternate content, information which is readily consumable and translatable by Braille devices and related technologies. (See *The AnyBrowser Pages* and the *Web Accessibility Initiative* for a detailed treatment of the subject.)

The goal of flexible design is not to ensure that every customer has access to the same experience, but that every customer has access to a complete and well designed experience. Customer-friendly design relies on websites degrading gracefully so that the experience can be delivered to a variety of customers, through a variety of means.

Guidelines for Flexible Design

The first step towards flexible design is distinguishing between content and presentation. Text is the least common denominator of web media. All browsers are capable of rendering text and text can be easily communicated to various supporting technologies like Braille devices. To reinforce this 'bottom line' media, we should separate the *meaning* of text from the *presentation* of text. HTML is a structural mark-up language, not a graphical mark-up language. This means that HTML should be used to *create relationships* between pieces of content. It does this by methods such as creating consistent headings and subheadings, emphasising words or phrases, determining the *relative* size of text and linking documents together. It should not be used to *control the appearance* of content, for two reasons:

1. It is not very good at it.
2. It is not capable of doing so in a manner that will degrade gracefully.

For example, using tables just as a layout tool can result in nonsense when a table is rendered purely as text rather than being graphically displayed. Likewise, tags like <blockquote> and <address> convey information about the text which they contain. If they are used simply to indent or emphasise text, they communicate the wrong message (particularly to accessibility devices).

The most effective way I have found for formatting textual content in a gracefully degrading fashion is through the use of *cascading style sheets.* Style sheets can be used, either within a document or by linking to an external document, to exert a tremendous amount of control over the appearance of different HTML page elements, for example the way <p>, <h2>, or <li> and other tags format the text which they contain. If a browser supports style sheets, the user gains the full benefit of the design; if not, the style sheet is ignored and the browser renders the tagged text in accordance with the HTML specification. Even though the visual formatting of the information is lost, its structure and value is preserved. This is, of course, the goal of designing for graceful degradation (see Meyer, 2000; Nielsen, 1997b).

Style sheets provide a tool for allowing text to degrade gracefully. Text itself provides a tool for allowing various media files to do the same. For example, images should always include a meaningful 'alt' attribute, which will display text to users without image support or who have images turned off. For an 'alt' attribute to be meaningful, it should fulfil the same purpose as the image. If the image is purely decorative, then the 'alt' attribute might simply specify the file name, dimensions (in pixels) and size (in KB) of the image, thus allowing the user to decide if the decoration is worth downloading. If the image is informative, not decorative, then the 'alt' attribute should contain the *meaning of the image*, not simply information *about* the image. The use of 'alt' attributes in images serves another important function. Normally, images on a page are not taken into account when a search engine indexes a page. The 'alt' attribute can thus raise a page's visibility by forcing engines to recognise that the page contains content (albeit visual) related to the search phrase.

If the image is a clickable element (for example, part of an image based navigation tool), then alternatives are even more

Figure 3.1: http://www.cdnow.com (March 2000)

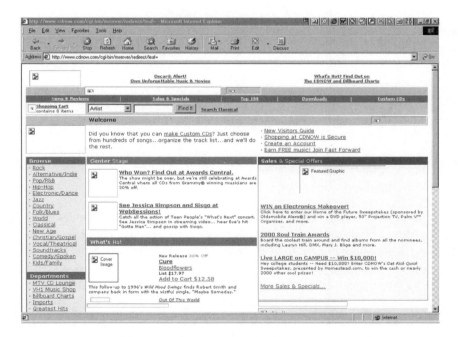

Figure 3.2: http://www.cdnow.com. No images (March 2000)

important. Figure 3.1 shows the home page of the music store, CD NOW. Figure 3.2 shows the same page, with images turned off.

The image map, which serves as the global navigation tool, contains no alternative text. As a result, the links to 'Video', 'Gifts', 'My CD NOW', 'Help' and the 'Cosmic Music Network' are not displayed. There are alternative text links to the first four listed, but they at the very bottom of the page which requires the customer to go hunting for them. There is *no alternative link* to the 'Cosmic Music Network', which presumably is the focus of a promotional effort since it has been given prime screen real estate. So, four out of the five global destinations are hidden and the fifth is simply absent.

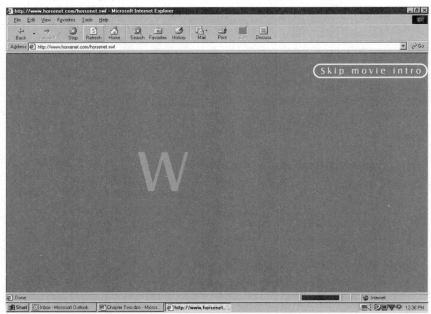

Figure 3.3: http://www.horsenet.com (February 2000)

Images are not the only kind of media files that demand alternatives. Designers using media files that require plug-ins (like Flash) should be even more aggressive in supplying alternative content. They should detect for the presence of the plug-in and, in its absence, redirect users to appropriate, alternative content. The dangers of not providing alternatives to media files are not limited to pages displaying poorly. A page without alternatives can alienate customers. For example, Horsenet.com uses a Flash animation on its front page. In December 1999, one of my students visited Horsenet.com. This student didn't have the plug-in so the page couldn't load. He hit the 'Back' button so Horsenet.com lost a potential sale. Just a few lines of code could have been used to check if the user's computer supported Flash and, if not, to redirect that user to a different page. It's hard to imagine a shop owner in the 'real world' installing doorknobs that could only be turned by customers who had a special, surgically implanted plug-in. Welcome to the inconvenience store!

Figure 3.3 shows the Horsenet.com website in the process of showing the Flash animation. The 'Skip Movie Intro' is just a tease — it is, in fact, a part of the animation. And no, they still haven't written that detection/redirect code.

Marshall McLuhan (1994) coined the phrase 'the medium is the message'. On one level, 'the medium is the message' means that the vehicle chosen for communication sends a 'meta-message' which is as expressive as the content of the communication. In the examples above, CD NOW and Horsenet.com have not made *technological* errors — they've made *customer service* errors. When an e-commerce company uses technology and multimedia judiciously and courteously (by providing alternatives), they send the message 'We want to improve your experience'. When the same company uses the same tools gratuitously and without regard to the limitations of the medium, they send the message 'Your custom is not desired'.

In addition to media files, scripts on a page require alternatives. If you use JavaScript, several precautions are recommended. Scripts are embedded in a web page between <script></script> tags. Like all tags, they will be ignored by browsers that don't understand them. Unfortunately, the content between the tags (lines of JavaScript code) will then be rendered as text. To get around this, be certain that scripts are enclosed in HTML comments (<!-- ... -->), which will hide the script from the browser. If the script was just 'bells and whistles', nothing more need be done. If, on the other hand, it provided some real piece of functionality, <noscript></noscript> tags should be used to provide an alternative. Also bear in mind that although JavaScript is widely supported, the support is often only partial. Program conservatively, and when using aspects of JavaScript which you know to be supported inconsistently, detect for the support before executing the script. Remember, there is no reason for a customer to trust a site's online payment system if every page comes up with a JavaScript error alert.

Beyond separating content from presentation and providing alternatives, designers need to adhere to standards set by the World Wide Web Consortium or equivalent body. For critical content and functionality, designers should not rely on browser specific HTML tags, like Navigator's <spacer> or Explorer's <label>. They are both useful tags (one for inserting white space and the other for annotating form elements) but they are not implemented by all browsers. Likewise, when writing JavaScript, the specifications of the international standard should be followed. Both Navigator and Explorer offer extensions to JavaScript which are not interoperable.

Part of adherence to standards means staying behind the cutting edge. Designers should utilise HTML 3.2 and JavaScript 1.1 as much as possible. It's a fact that 34% of users are running Internet Explorer 4 or Netscape Navigator 4, which only partially support the HTML 4.0 specification. Another 3% are running even earlier versions that only support HTML 3.2 and may not support style sheets, JavaScript, Java, plug-ins, frames or animated GIF files (Upsdell, 2000). Web TV, PDA and other devices offer even lower levels of support.

When a site does require functionality only offered by HTML 4.0 and JavaScript 1.2/1.3, designers must make certain they include an alternative means of delivering the content. Likewise, special media that require plug-ins should be used sparingly and media types that are well supported should be chosen, not simply the 'latest and greatest' technology. Designers should be aware that plug-ins are not as common as is commonly believed. As of December 1999:

- 32% of users did not have AVI
- 48% of users did not have QuickTime
- 63% of users did not have ShockWave
- 61% of users did not have RealPlayer G2
- 64% of users did not have Acrobat Reader (Upsdell, 2000).

One of the most critical aspects of flexible design is in creating websites that perform well in a variety of monitor configurations. Most designers have high resolution monitors set to 1024 x 768 pixels or higher. But 56% of e-commerce customers have monitors set to 800 x 600 and another 11% have monitors set to 640 x 480 (Upsdell, 2000). Figures 3.4–3.6 show the impact that resolution can have on a page.

Figure 3.4: http://www.gap.com. Resolution 1024 x 768 (February 2000)

Figure 3.5: http://www.gap.com. Resolution 800 x 600 (February 2000)

Figure 3.6: http://www,gap.com. Resolution 640 x 480 (February 2000)

Figure 3.4 shows the full Gap homepage at 1024 x 768 resolution. However, only three out of ten users use that resolution. Six out of ten visitors will see Figure 3.5, which means that unless they scroll down, they cannot see the links to the site directory, information about the company, contact information, the first time user's instruction manual, the privacy policy, security policy and terms of use. For the one in ten users viewing the page at 640 x 480 (Figure 3.6), the links related to returns and current sale offers are also obscured. More importantly, seven out of ten users cannot see the most important feature — 'Buy This Item' (Figure 3.7).

In addition to screen resolution (for more on the subject see Niederst, 1999), designers must take into account colour depth. In general, personal computers offer three levels of colour support:

- 8-bit colour (256 colours, 8% of web users)
- 16-bit colour (64K colours, 54% of users)
- 24-bit colour (16 million colours, 38% of users) (Upsdell, 2000).

There are only 216 colours, called the 'web palate', which will appear in a predictable fashion in all three colour environments. (There are 216, not 256, because the remaining 40 display differently on Mac OS and Windows machines.) Other colours will change in appearance or 'dither' when viewed in a lower depth environment. As much as possible, stay within this palette when designing your graphics and page colour schemes.

To deliver flexible pages, colours should contrast by *value*, not *hue*. Designing within the web palate can save a designer a lot of headache, but what if the monitor can't render colour at all? When a web page is viewed through a grey-scale monitor, the colours are rendered according to their value (brightness). Yet many web pages use text/background colours with a similar value and contrasting hues (colour). When viewed in full colour, the contrast is high. But in a value only environment, the contrast is negligible and the text becomes illegible. Choosing colours by value rather than hue will also make pages more accessible to colour-blind users. (See *lynda.com,* http://www.lynda.com, for free web palette colour charts based on hue and value.)

Figure 3.7: http://www.gap.com. Resolution 800 x 600 or lower

(February 2000)

Finally, HTML tables and horizontal rules can be specified in absolute terms (number of pixels) or relative terms (percentage of parent element). Designers should use relative sizing if at all possible to allow for different screen resolutions and window sizes. When using absolute measurements, it is important to keep the horizontal axis small. This is because customers are reluctant to scroll down a page and twice as reluctant to scroll right. Likewise, designers should assume that text will wrap according to the size of the display area and design so that the meaning of content is preserved when the final layout changes in unexpected ways. To its credit, Gap sets the width of the table holding the page's content to 554 pixels, so that even at 640 x 480, I didn't need to scroll right. However, that number assumes that users will have the window maximised to the full screen. If a user is shopping at Gap in a smaller window, the absolute sizing means that content gets cut off.

As with speed, a commitment to flexibility goes a long way towards creating a more customer-friendly site. It is important that design teams create a house style guide and enforce it globally with style sheets, allowing content creators to focus on content and not format. Likewise, there should be meaningful alternative content provided for all multimedia and programmatic content. Companies should choose a technology cut-off point (colour depth, screen resolution, browser version, etc.) and consistently design within those limits. Finally, sites should be tested through a variety of browsers, on different platforms, with different colour depths and screen resolutions.

CHAPTER 4:

Designing for Usability

Why Usability is Important
In the previous two chapters, I focused on techniques for delivering web content in a fast and flexible manner. Speed and flexibility are of critical importance to e-commerce — if a customer leaves a site because it is too slow, or if she cannot make use of the site's content and functionality due to technical incompatibility, the rest of the site's design is irrelevant. Assuming that the design team has met these straightforward technical goals, it must now turn to a more sophisticated and humanistic challenge: designing for usability.

In a recent *Information Week* article (Nielsen and Norman, 2000), Jakob Nielsen and Donald A. Norman wrote that the medium of the web puts the 'user experience of the site first, purchase and payment second ... Only if a site is extremely easy to use will anybody bother staying around.' This chapter provides a set of general guidelines for building sites that are 'extremely easy to use'. The goal is simple: to not only get customers to 'stay around', but to provide such a positive user experience that they will be eager to return.

Nielsen, Norman and the *Macintosh Human Interface Guidelines*
The guidelines in this chapter draw heavily upon three classic usability texts (none of which, it should be noted, were written with an eye specifically on the web):

- Norman's *The Design of Everyday Things* (1998)
- Nielsen's *Usability Engineering* (1993)
- Apple Computer's *Macintosh Human Interface Guidelines* (1995).

The Design of Everyday Things is a manifesto on what might be called 'fundamental' usability design principles. The book has nothing to do with the web and discusses computers only briefly. It focuses on two simple issues: how people use things, and how designers can thus make things easier to use. As the title suggests, the work examines the usability of common items — doors, light switches and the like. Although it might not seem so at first, this focus provides an ideal foundation for e-commerce usability design. The goal of consumer-oriented e-commerce is to bring the web into the everyday lives of everyday people. The internet is shrouded in mystery, jargon and technological intimidation. Designers must seek to make web based commerce as accessible and familiar as a toothbrush.

Norman teaches us that designers can enhance the usability of a product by adhering to a handful of ideas:

- maximise visibility: when looking at an object, it should be obvious to the user what actions he can take. Likewise, the results of an action should be clearly visible
- maximise simplicity: it is the goal of the designer to make tasks as simple as possible
- take advantage of internal knowledge: users approach a task with a lifetime of learning behind them. Designers should create systems which allow users to apply previous learning
- make external knowledge as accessible as possible: simple, everyday items (like a website, I would argue) should not require a user's manual. Instead, Norman recommends 'teaching' users through:
  - good mapping techniques (such as relating the appearance of controls to what they do, how they are to be used, etc.)
  - the use of constraints (the limitations built into the material or design e.g. the height of a dining table constrains sitting)
  - the use of affordances (the possibilities built into the material of design e.g. the width and sturdiness of the same table affords laying out items, such as a meal).
- assume that there will be errors: Murphy's law is the designer's gospel — if something can go wrong, it will. Designers should include systems both for error prevention and error recovery
- promote and adhere to standards: earlier, I argued for adherence to standards because computers require it for interoperability. Norman points out that humans require it as well. Standards take advantage of previous learning and impose cultural constraints to promote correct user action.

The focus of *Usability Engineering* is much closer to the present work than *The Design of Everyday Things*. While it does not deal explicitly with the web, it is written for professional developers of computer systems and user interfaces. And as I've argued in previous chapters, an e-commerce website is a user interface, so the advice in *Usability Engineering* is very relevant. Nielsen defines the usability of a system as a combination of:

- how easy the system is to learn
- how efficiently a person who has learned the system can actually use it
- how easy it is for a user to retain knowledge between sessions
- how error proof and error tolerant the system is
- how much users actually like to use the system.

Nielsen offers designers and developers a guide to usability heuristics which are similar to Norman's principles above. Nielsen encourages:

- simplifying the interface as much as possible by removing unnecessary information and controls
- engaging the user in a natural dialogue which matches the interface to the task, possibly through the use of metaphor
- using visual design principles to clarify the structure and meaning of information and controls
- using the user's language and taking the user's point of view (users should not need to learn a new vocabulary, nor should they need to guess what the designer was thinking)
- relieving the user of the burden of memory (for example, using menus rather than requiring the user to enter in a memorised command)
- being as consistent as possible (in screen layout, menu layout, labelling conventions, etc.)
- providing feedback both when errors are made and when things are going well (progress indicators)
- providing clearly marked exits, shortcuts and help functions.

Finally, the *Macintosh Human Interface Guidelines* (which, like *Usability Engineering,* focuses on general interface design not the web) lays down a set of principles for Macintosh application developers. Its other strengths and weaknesses aside, the Macintosh interface is generally considered by users to be an accessible, forgiving and pleasant environment in which to work, largely due to adherence to these principles. Apple Computer Inc. suggests that the user's experience will be improved if designers:

- add leverage to a user's knowledge of the 'real world' through the use of metaphors
- allow people to feel in control of their actions by directly manipulating objects on the screen
- encourage a 'noun then verb' model of user action, in which users select a screen object (noun) and then do something with it (verb)
- maintain consistency within and between applications
- meet the user's expectations
- actively engage the user and put the user in control
- provide useful feedback
- allow users to undo actions
- build systems for error prevention and recovery
- organise content following the basic principles of visual design.

Guidelines for Usable Design

Using these three texts, we can lay down four key guidelines for usable, and therefore customer-friendly, design:

1. Promote natural, intuitive learning.
2. Make controls, their functions and their results clearly visible.
3. Take advantage of the natural constraints and affordances of web objects.
4. Be flexible and allow users to undo mistakes.

Promote natural, intuitive learning

To start with, a customer-friendly site should promote natural learning. A customer should 'learn' how to use a site in a quick, natural and intuitive manner and not have to read paragraph after paragraph of instructions. For example, a field in a form should not have 100 words of directions. Instead, it should have an unambiguous label and, if necessary, a default value to clarify what is required. Customers will learn more quickly by example than by instruction. Under no circumstances should a 'user manual' be required. If a manual *is* needed, the site is too difficult to use. Customers visit a retail web site to research products and then, hopefully, purchase products. They do not come to a site to learn a new 'application'. For example, if a customer wants to buy a pair of men's jeans from Gap, it should be a five step process:

1. Select menswear.

2. Select jeans from a category list.
3. Pick a style, and click 'Buy'.
4. Select details like size, colour and quantity.
5. Enter in billing and shipping information.

Five steps, five pages, five minutes, deal closed, happy customer, happy store. It is the designer's job to keep this set of tasks as simple as possible and make it unmistakably clear to customers how they are to accomplish each task. Actually, although the pages are often cluttered and content is not very well prioritised, buying at Gap.com is a fairly straightforward process. Why, then, does the Gap website (Figure 4.1) have a thirty page pop-up user manual?

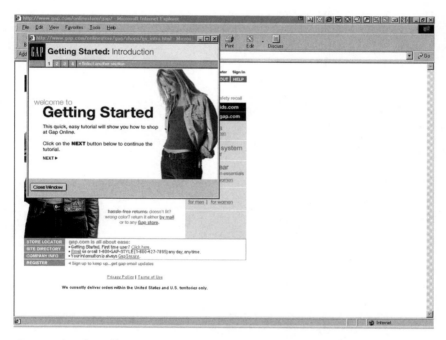

Figure 4.1: http://www.gap.com. Pop-up user manual (February 2000)

Why does entering billing and mailing information require nine pages of explanation (not including the security statement, which is elsewhere in the site)? Why does buying a t-shirt for a friend require fifteen pages of explanation, including complex explanations for each operable feature (Figure 4.2)?

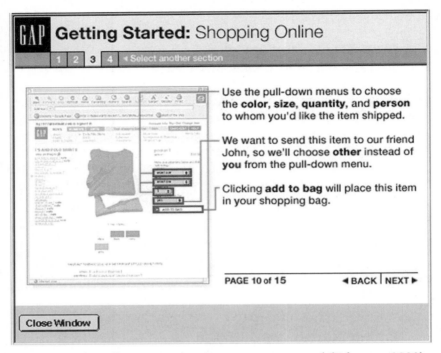

Figure 4.2: http://www.gap.com. Pop-up user manual (February 2000)

On the one hand, the designers at Gap are to be praised. They cared enough about the customer to put together this thirty-page subsite. Likewise, the 'buy a t-shirt' tutorial demonstrates that they are thinking in use-cases, which is good. But their efforts are misdirected. Customers visit to buy new outfits, not to learn a new system. The link that leads to the manual says 'gap.com is all about ease ... First time user? Click here'. As stated above, a website built for ease of use should not require a manual.

Manuals intimidate and distract users. Customers should be thinking 'What would I like to buy?', not 'I hope I can remember all this ...'. Manuals are a burden for the customer, especially a newcomer to e-commerce who feels obliged to 'follow the rules'. By turning a five-click shopping trip into a thirty-page tutorial we make certain that first-time users don't become second-time users.

Manuals distract designers as well. As we learned from Nielsen, Norman and Apple Inc., customers should not be asked to remember anything; the information required for each step should be at their finger tips when needed. Designers should focus on fine-tuning the content and presentation of the interface itself, not on creating subsites that explain the interface. The time spent building the Gap manual should have been spent refining content and developing a more usable interface, especially since most customers do not read instructions anyway (see Hurst, 1999).

Notice that the user manual doesn't need a set of instructions. That's because its operation is simple:

- there is a clear title at the top
- to jump to a new section, users click 1, 2, 3 or 4. Right next to each number is a little arrow and three unambiguous words 'Select another section'
- the main area is consistent — an image on the left and text on the right
- below the text is a status message telling customers where they are (e.g. 'Page 10 of 15') and two arrows telling them where they can go ('Back' and 'Next')
- the only other possible action is to leave the manual, clearly marked by the 'Close Window' button.

The design of the user manual is exemplary. If every page in an online store was this easy, there would be no user manuals. Every page *should* be this easy! Clear and accurate labels, a high profile, simple-to-use navigation tool, prominent uncluttered content, feedback to let customers know where they are and visible, unambiguous controls are all far more valuable than explicit instructions. Easy to use means easy to learn. As noted above, it is fairly easy to shop at Gap.com. Veteran customers will dive right in and get their jeans. All the manual does is intimidate first-time shoppers, who read it because they are uncertain and come away thinking the site is more difficult than it really is.

An important part of promoting natural learning is promoting natural action. Designers need to make controls, their functions and their results clearly visible. Not counting things like Java applets, which are applications in themselves, there are only a few controls that can be placed on web pages: links, buttons and form elements such as checkboxes, radio buttons and text fields. These controls should be immediately recognisable as controls, their function should be predictable and, when used, the result should be immediate and obvious. For example, links should look like links and things that are not links should not. Novice web users quickly learn the conventions of the web and e-merchants are well advised to reinforce this learning. While style sheets make it possible to remove the tell-tale underline from text links, this makes it difficult for the customer to recognise the text as a control. Likewise, image maps do not always demonstrate their active nature clearly. If a site uses non-standard link formats, it should utilise other clues (a button-like appearance, positioning, labels etc.) to inform the customer that what they see is not just text or an image, but a control element. A page should, of course, always contain standard alternatives for non-standard elements. On the flip side, designers should never use underlining as a form of emphasis. When customers encounter underlined text, they assume it is a link, even if other links on the page are not underlined.

Similarly, if an object looks like a button or a form element, it should act like a button or a form element. Control elements are not decoration and elements that do nothing will only confuse and irritate users. Furthermore, the function of an element (and the result of using it) should be predictable and visible. Worse than a button that does nothing is a button that acts in unexpected ways. Labels should be unambiguous and situated close to the element referenced.

Figure 4.3 shows the shopping basket at MarthaStewart.com. Quite frankly, this shopping cart is a usability nightmare.

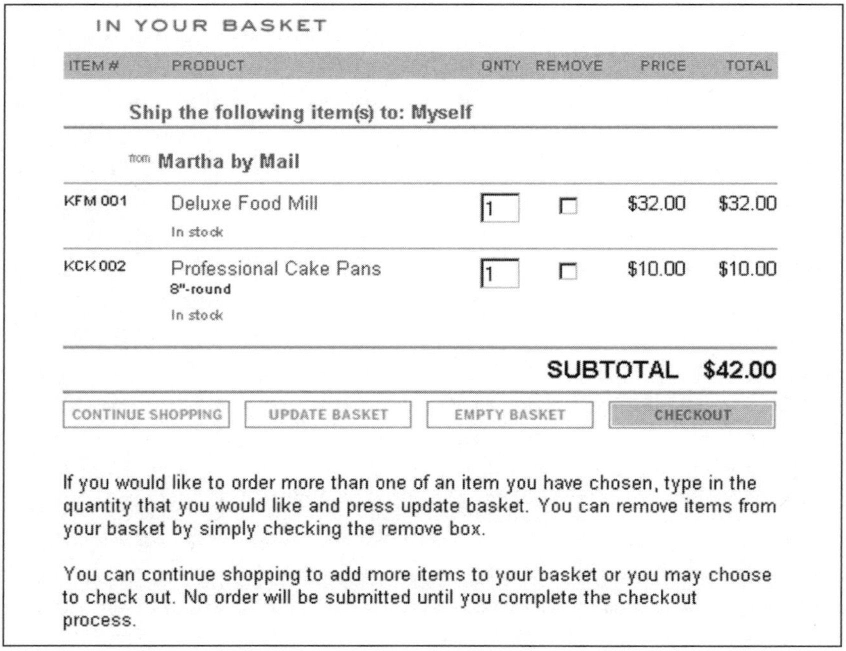

IN YOUR BASKET						
ITEM #	PRODUCT		QNTY	REMOVE	PRICE	TOTAL
	Ship the following item(s) to: Myself					
	from Martha by Mail					
KFM 001	Deluxe Food Mill In stock		1	☐	$32.00	$32.00
KCK 002	Professional Cake Pans 8"-round In stock		1	☐	$10.00	$10.00
					SUBTOTAL	$42.00

CONTINUE SHOPPING   UPDATE BASKET   EMPTY BASKET   CHECKOUT

If you would like to order more than one of an item you have chosen, type in the quantity that you would like and press update basket. You can remove items from your basket by simply checking the remove box.

You can continue shopping to add more items to your basket or you may choose to check out. No order will be submitted until you complete the checkout process.

Figure 4.3: http://www.marthastewart.com. Close-up of shopping basket (February 2000)

Both the labels (which customers will use) and the instructions (which most customers won't use) are too far away from the table elements to which they refer. The distance itself can be overcome, but not the intervening visual elements. The labels should be lowered so that they can more directly reference the table elements and should be rewritten so that the instructions are not required at all. For example, the label 'Qnty' is unnecessarily abbreviated, creating another layer of work for the customer. The lengthy instructions for the operation of the 'Qnty' box should be replaced with a more exact label. Next to the 'Qnty' box is a checkbox with the label 'Remove'. As with 'Qnty,' this is unnecessarily abbreviated and should read 'Check to remove'.

The 'Remove' box is a particularly poorly designed feature. The instructions say 'You can remove items from your basket by simply checking the remove box'. While the directions for 'Qnty' were superfluous, the directions for 'Remove' are just plain wrong. 'Simply' implies that the item is deleted by just checking the box, yet when the box is checked, the item remains (no visible result). In actuality, customers must also click the 'Update Basket' button, although nowhere is this indicated. So customers are left to figure out the mechanism on their own. A customer thinks 'The box has been checked, but the cake pan is still there. Maybe it goes away when I leave the page?' So the customer clicks 'Continue Shopping', finds a nice set of napkin rings and returns to the cart page. The cake pan is still there! They check the box again and look around for something to make the operation stick. They know that 'Continue Shopping' doesn't work (already tried that) and 'Checkout' doesn't seem to be a good bet (that's one label that is clear). The customer is thus left with two options — 'Update Basket' or 'Empty Basket'. Now, which verb seems more appropriate to the job of removing items? The user clicks and they see Figure 4.4.

The customer did not make a bad choice. The customer was presented with bad options. 'Empty Basket' should read 'Remove All Items' and 'Update Basket' should simply say 'Make Changes' ('update' is too technical). So now the basket is empty, the e-cash register is empty and, a few clicks from now, Martha Stewart's customer is someone else's customer in an e-store where putting an item back is not a puzzle to be solved.

Usability is a concept that is revisited in each of the chapters to follow, as it is absolutely critical to building a successful, customer-friendly web site. The various interfaces discussed throughout the rest of the book — navigation, search, transactions and community — are all tools presented to the customer. If the function, and thus operation, of these tools is easily accessible, customers can complete their chosen task and go away happy. If they are not designed for usability, customers will 'fail'. Where customers fail, companies follow.

For interested readers, there are several excellent resources available on the subject of usability in addition to Norman, Nielsen and Apple's works noted above. Recently, Nielsen (2000a) published *Designing Web Usability,* which is certain to become a canonical work on the subject. Many of the ideas discussed in the book can also be found in an earlier form at Jakob Nielsen's website, *useit.com.* Other excellent online sources include Keith Instone's *Usable Web,* a clearinghouse which boasts over 800 related links, and the usability interviews at *Web Word.*

Figure 4.4: http://www.marthastewart.com. Close-up of shopping basket (February 2000)

CHAPTER 5:

Navigation Interfaces

The Role of Navigation in a Commercial Environment

To understand the role of navigation in e-commerce, it is useful to return to the argument made in Chapter 1, namely that an e-commerce site is an environment. An environment is a space in which individuals can interact with objects and with each other, where individuals can follow the lay of the land or else the trails made by others, and in which individuals can acclimate themselves to create a 'sense of place'. It's also a place where it is often easy to get lost.

The navigation interface of an e-commerce site is a set of tools (e.g. links, icons, labels, bits of content) which allows the customer to take advantage of the environment without getting lost. It should:

- allow customers to easily find the objects that populate the space (products, information, shopping aids, etc.)
- allow customers to find other human beings (other users, store staff, etc.)
- allow customers to follow both the lay of the land and explicit trails (by offering consistent, well labelled and obvious paths)
- allow customers to feel at home (by providing access to information about the site, store policies, the company, etc.).

In meeting these goals, a designer goes a long way towards insuring that customers don't get lost, or at least not for long. Fleming (1998) offers a similar summary of the key navigation functionality required in a commercial environment. She writes that the site should help users understand where they are, where they can go to and where they came from, as well as how to find products, information and key functional elements (like the check-out).

Navigation is important to the success of an e-commerce site for four simple reasons:

1. If customers can't find the product or service, it doesn't exist.
2. If customers can't find information on a product or service, they don't know if it meets their needs.
3. If customers can't find information on store policies (privacy, security, returns, etc.) they don't know if they can trust the company.
4. If customers can't find the check-out, they can't buy.

This chapter offers both guidelines for designing navigational systems and critiques of the navigational systems of several e-commerce sites.

Guidelines for Navigation Design

In general, e-commerce navigational systems support a combination of three different levels of navigation (which are then supplemented with search tools):

* global
* local
* inline.

Global navigation

This is used to provide access to the major sections of the site from every page. Note that the definition of 'major' will be different for every site. The scope might be quite broad (online store, news, chat and bulletin-boards); moderate (books, music, movies) or very narrow (fiction, history, DIY). There is no right scope. Rather, the specificity of global links should depend on the content within the site. The important thing is for designers to strive for *consistency*. Global navigation systems should provide links to areas of the site of equivalent scope (no matter what level of specificity that may be) and they should provide the same global links on every page. When the global system fluctuates from page to page, it ceases to be global.

For a consumer e-commerce environment, the goal of global navigation design should be to:

* allow customers to easily switch between the major sections of the site
* provide ready access to 'meta' information (privacy, security, shipping and returns information, the contents of the shopping cart, etc.)
* make it easy to find the check-out page.

Local navigation

Local navigation systems provide links to pages within a particular section of the site. For example, if the global system included a link to a clothing section, the clothing section might include local links to 'his' and 'hers', or to 'jeans' and 'dresses,' etc. Local systems should be kept local; customers shopping for circular saws don't need detailed links to every product category in the clothing section. Again, consistency is important and helps to maintain the customer's sense of location. If the circular saw shopper was suddenly presented with links to shoes, she may think she took a wrong turn.

The goal of local navigation tools should be to make it easy for customers:

- to locate individual products/services
- to locate more information about individual products/services
- to browse groups of related products/services.

Inline navigation

Sometimes known as *ad hoc* navigation, inline navigation consists of hyperlinks embedded into other content rather than into a formal navigational element. Good uses of inline navigation include links to supporting information (like a pop-up glossary of computer terms) or to related products and services elsewhere in the site. Inline linking can greatly improve the customer interface and is a powerful promotional tool, but it should be used with caution. Too many links will make it difficult for the customer to consume the content of a page, a bit like listening to a speaker who constantly interrupts himself. Also, inline links need to be very well contextualised; before the customer abandons the current content to follow the link, she should have a clear idea of where the link is going.

Guidelines

Whether a designer is creating a global, local or inline system, there are certain guidelines to follow if the system is going to create value and address the customer's previously defined need for speed, flexibility and usability.

First, customer-friendly navigation is consistent, allowing users to use previously acquired knowledge. To help customers recognise (and thus use) navigational elements, the elements should:

- have a consistent visual appearance
- be located on the page in a consistent manner
- have consistent labels to identify destinations.

Also, as noted before, hyperlinks should always look like hyperlinks; non hyperlinks should not. In other words, elements should not only be consistent with each other on a site, but also with wider web conventions.

Second, while is important that decorative images degrade gracefully, the flexible presentation of functional images (such as a navigation button, icon or image-map) is ten times as important. While local and inline navigation tend to be text based, many sites use graphical global elements. It is vital that:

- <alt> tags are used for all images
- text labels (also hyperlinked) are provided for every icon
- an alternative text-based navigation tool is provided for all image-map links.

Also, as more and more e-commerce sites use JavaScript and Dynamic HTML to create very slick navigational tools, it becomes increasingly important that designers make use of browser detects/redirects so that customers see the site which is appropriate to their means of consumption. Designers should also always provide vanilla HTML alternatives to programmatic elements.

Third, navigation should be comprehensive, but still clean and clear. It is important that a customer can find all of the information on a site, but not all on the same page. The overall navigation system should be comprehensive, but the navigational choices on a given page should be limited to global destinations, relevant local destinations and extremely relevant inline choices. Likewise, labels should indicate in an unambiguous fashion where a given link will take the customer. Clarity can also be enhanced by *not* linking to the page the customer is currently viewing. Rather, the customer's current location within both the global and local space should be indicated (for example, with a greyed out link).

There are a number of excellent sources of information on navigation design, including Fleming's (1998) book cited above. In particular, Chapters 2 and 7 complement the present discussion of navigation well. Also, since successful navigation systems are built on top of robust information architectures, I will again recommend a careful reading of Rosenfeld and Morville (1998), particularly Chapters 4 and 5. Online, see C|Net's *Spotlight on Navigation Design* and *Webreview.com's* navigation section.

Navigation Critiques

The rest of this chapter looks at the navigational systems of various e-commerce sites, highlighting how well the systems met (or failed to meet) the goals and guidelines outlined above.

Garden.com (Figures 5.1–5.4) sells a large variety of gardening products, maintains an interactive garden planner, hosts a chat based community and publishes a gardening magazine.

Since garden.com provides four diverse services, the global navigation is very broad in scope. At the top of the page (see Figure 5.1) there are links pointing to the shop, the planner, the community and the magazine. There are also links (in an image-map in the upper right-hand corner) going to 'our privacy pledge', 'join here for free!', 'member's sign in', 'I forgot my password' and 'join garden.com now!' At the bottom of the page (see Figure 5.2) the global elements continue, with 'about garden.com', 'customer solutions' and a toll-free phone number (which looks the same as the links). At the very bottom there is a collection of text links which include 'magazine', 'shopping', 'community', 'design a garden', 'about us', 'jobs', 'advertising' and 'feedback'. On the homepage, the entire left margin is devoted to search tools.

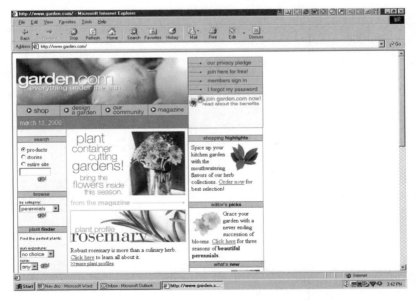

Figure 5.1: http://www.garden.com. Top of homepage (March 2000)

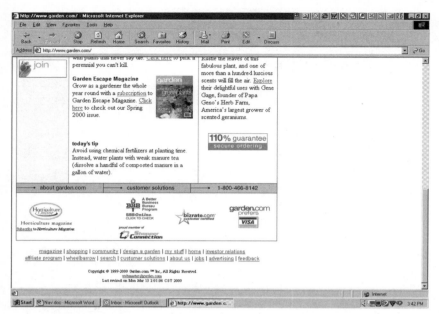

Figure 5.2: http://www.garden.com. Bottom of homepage (March 2000)

Customers clicking on 'shop' (see Figure 5.3) will see the search tools pushed down the page and replaced with the local navigation system. This includes links to 'home', the 'wheelbarrow' and a 'help desk', as well as links to sales, gifts, payment information, etc. The central content of the 'shop page' is a menu of products, each item of which expands into a more detailed menu when clicked. Actual product pages (see Figure 5.4) retain the global and local navigation choices. They also offer a 'breadcrumb' trail, such as 'shopping/seeds/perennial flowers' allowing customers to move up and down the hierarchy of products.

Some aspects of Garden.com's navigation are quite good. The breadcrumb trail is a very effective means of allowing customers to browse groups of items at different levels of specificity. The customer's current location is well marked in both the global and local navigation elements. There is also a consistent use of navigational tools from page to page. However, other aspects of the system are very poor. Although Garden.com addressed the important need for page-to-page consistency, there is little consistency between elements on the same page, particularly in terms of labels. From 'why buy' to 'customer solutions', the labels are often obscure and vary greatly in style. They are also often redundant — 'join here for free!' and 'join garden.com now!' appear an inch from each other at the top of every page. The redundancy and the inconsistency of style serve both to clutter the pages and weaken the navigational system.

Figure 5.3: http://www.garden.com. Shopping section (March 2000)

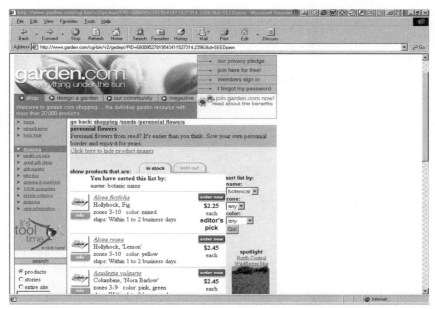

Figure 5.4: http://www.garden.com. Product page (March 2000)

More importantly, the navigation system does not degrade gracefully. There are <alt> tags for 'shop', 'garden planner', 'community' and 'magazine', but not for the other five links in the image-map in the upper right-hand corner of the page. (Actually, there is one <alt> tag for the image-map, but it makes matters worse. When viewed without images, the words 'log in' appear at the top of the image-map, which actually links to the privacy statement.) The text links at the bottom of the page cannot do their job as alternates very well because the labels are sometimes different. For example, it took me a while to realise that 'my stuff' was the same as 'members sign in' above.

Finally, although the link to the privacy statement is quite prominent, the links to security information and to the check-out page are not. In fact the only way to get to the check-out counter is through the 'wheelbarrow' which itself is not that visible, especially when compared to the big 'join garden.com now!' sign. Garden.com is off to a good start, makes appropriate use of inline links and boasts some really great features, like the ability to sort a list of products by a variety of parameters (alphabetically, by price, etc.). Just the same, the global and local navigational systems would be greatly improved by:

- adopting a consistent editorial voice and style for labels (rather than jumping between words and phrases, between nouns and verbs and between chatty slang and business jargon)
- adding <alt> tags to all graphical navigation elements
- reconciling the text links with their graphical equivalents
- removing redundant links and giving greater prominence to the 'wheelbarrow', secure ordering information and the check-out page.

The Discovery Store provides top-of-page, global links to:

- sister services within Discovery.com
- the home page
- the 'Web Express'
- 'My Discovery' (Figure 5.5).

There is also a very visible bar linking to 'Privacy/Security', 'Customer Service', and 'View Cart'. The side bar contains a search box, links to product categories and links to other e-stores (although their relationship to the Discovery Store is not made clear).

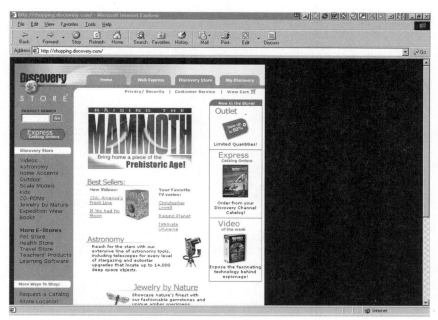

Figure 5.5: http://shopping.discovery.com. Top of home page (March 2000)

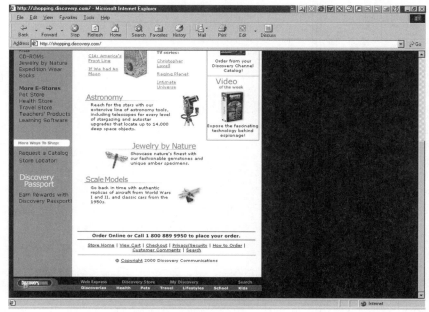

Figure 5.6: http://shopping.discovery.com. Bottom of home page (March 2000)

The bottom of the page (Figure 5.6) contains a text menu that echoes the important shop links above. There is also a full graphic navigation bar going to a variety of subject headings ('Health', 'Pets', 'Travel' etc.).

The best navigational feature on this home page is the prominence of the privacy/security link, the shopping cart and the customer service link — three key customer concerns. The labels chosen for these links are consistently professional (rather than chatty) and familiar (customer 'service' rather than customer 'solutions'). The rest of the system leaves much to be desired. For example, the product categories should be refined. Currently, the categories are a mixture of subject areas (e.g. 'Astronomy'), product types ('CD-ROMS') and audiences ('Kids'). This kind of inconsistency makes it difficult to choose a path — for example where do you click for a documentary on the solar system aimed at 8–11 year olds?

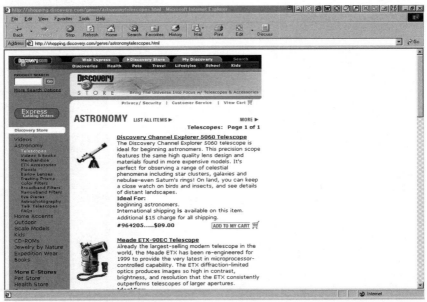

Figure 5.7: http://shopping.discovery.com. Top of product page (March 2000)

Individual product pages (like Figure 5.7) within the site are strong. The prominence of the links to privacy, security, customer service and shopping cart is maintained. Local navigation options are presented cleanly in the form of an indented menu on the left. The 'Buy' button is very prominent and located next to each item.

The only navigational difficulty within the product pages is that the link to the check-out page is hidden at the bottom of the page (see Figure 5.8).

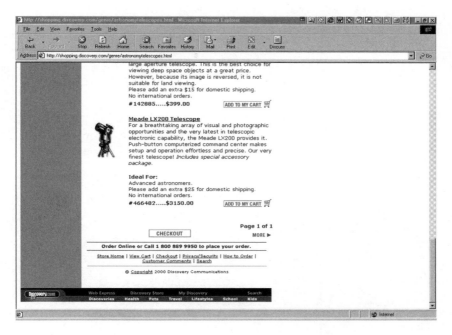

Figure 5.8: http://shopping.discovery.com. Bottom of product page (March 2000)

Despite the criticisms presented above, both Garden.com and the Discovery Store do a good job in creating a customer-friendly navigation system, especially considering the volume of (valuable) information each site provides. One of the reasons for their success is that they are consistent with the conventions of most of the rest of the commercial web: global navigation at the top, local to the left and breadcrumbs and indented menus. Although it can be criticised as dull, adhering to these *de facto* standards allows customers to ignore the navigational system and get on with what-ever they came to the site to do. When navigating a physical space, people want to look at the scenery and 'experience' the space. They don't want to watch each step carefully. The same is true online. The best navigation systems are invisible.

The next critique shows a gimmicky navigational theme that hogs the customer's attention at the expense of the site's actual content. The entrance to The Mall instructs customers to read about the site while they wait for the 'elevator' to load (Figure 5.9). Let this sink in. The first experience of every customer is thus being forced to wait for an elevator. Why should anyone have to wait for an elevator in cyberspace? While the impatient customer has already hit her back button, the more dedicated individual reads that:

- the site was designed to blend function with form (great)
- 'the architects have blended ground and sky in a graceful display' (not sure what that means)
- 'fully functional in the new transport technology, you will be molecularly transported from the mall elevator to the interior of the merchant's unit with a click of your mouse on the mall map'.

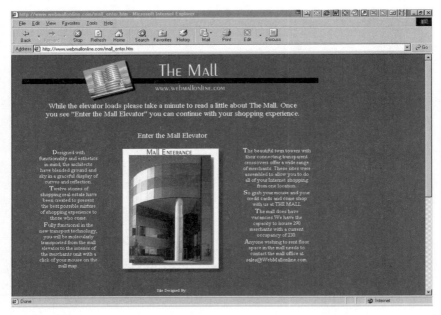

Figure 5.9: http://www.webmallonline.com. Entrance (March 2000)

After waiting patiently for the 'molecular transportation' device, the customer is shown Figure 5.10.

The text in the central panel tells the customer to click on the floor of choice. How is a customer to do this? Hovering over the buttons will trigger explanatory phrases to pop-up ('Travel and Airlines', 'Sports', etc.), but the customer doesn't know that unless he musters up the courage to blindly jab at one of the (for all practical purposes) unlabelled buttons. Half of the screen is blank grey so why rely on pop-up messages when a simple legend would do the job? Better still, why not simply skip the elevator and help the customer get as quickly as possible into a shop?

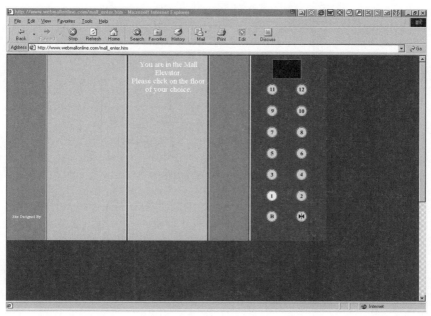

Figure 5.10: http://www.webmallonline.com. Elevator (March 2000)

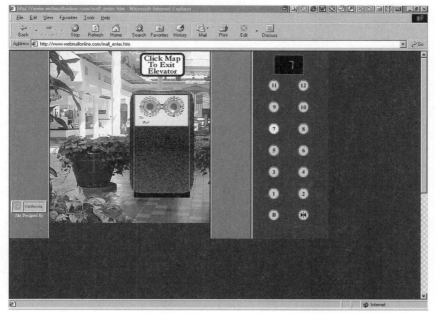

Figure 5.11: http://www.webmallonline.com. 7th floor (March 2000)

Imagine that a customer clicks '7' which is for travel services. Figure 5.11 appears.

The legend tells customers to click on the map to leave the elevator. Why should they? The map does not indicate what merchants are on this floor, nor does it even confirm that the customer is in the right department. Assuming the customer clicks on the map anyway, he sees Figure 5.12.

Finally the customer arrives at the place where a click of the button on the mall map will take them to a store. Actually, the map does nothing. Repeat, it serves no function whatsoever. Customers actually need to click on the *legend* of the map, a set of simple text links. Clicking one will bring you to the actual company website (say www.alaskaairlines.com) with no way of returning to The Mall. The graphics are pretty, the JavaScript which runs the show is very cleverly programmed. But why force customers to move through this elaborate, confusing and ultimately unnecessary 'virtual reality'? The role of navigation is to support content. The Mall presents customers with navigation as content (and nothing else).

Figure 5.12: http://www.webmallonline.com On the 7th floor (March 2000)

CHAPTER 6:

Search Interfaces

The Role of Search Tools in a Commercial Environment

Over the past several years I have observed people approaching the web in one of two manners — either from a 'pedestrian' perspective, or from a 'bird's eye' perspective. To use the internet in a pedestrian manner is to see cyberspace as a landscape to be navigated, a place to go. A bird's eye approach looks upon the same space as an object or group of objects to be manipulated.

Surfing is an irritating word but a very accurate description of the pedestrian approach to the web. Oceanic surfers follow the topology of the water, web surfers follow the topology of the web. The pedestrian user is operating on 'street level', navigating cyberspace as it has been created by designers and other users, moving from link to link to reach a destination. To meet the needs of pedestrian users, designers must pay attention to the navigational interface as discussed in the previous chapter.

Search engines are the tools of bird's eye web use. Rather than navigating cyberspace the *place*, search engines, like surfers, manipulate cyberspace the *object*, by filtering, editing and condensing it to serve their needs and wants. Rather than reinforcing the notion of a virtual geography, searching the web supports a different vision, namely that the web is not a collection of places but a collection of things. Addressing the needs of bird's eye web users through a powerful search interface is important, because the majority of web users take this approach. Nielsen (1997c) reports that more than half of all web users are search dominant.

Why do customers prefer to search, rather than navigate, the commercial web? One reason may be need, as the great majority of commercial sites suffer from poor information architecture and navigation systems. Another reason may be, simply, that it is more accurate to view systems like the web as collections of information.

The most important reason, however, is that navigation is simply not enough to address all of the ways in which customers seek information. Rosenfeld and Morville (1998) describe a number of ways in which people trawl an information space.

These include:

- searching for known items ('I want the *Graceland* album by Paul Simon')
- existence searching ('Is there a folk/pop singer named "Simon"?')
- exploratory searching ('I liked the back-up singers in *Graceland*. I want to know more about South African music')
- comprehensive research ('I want to assemble the authoritative Paul Simon album collection, and any associated interviews and reviews').

Each of these information needs will require a combination of searching and navigating behaviours and each is a plausible use-case for an e-commerce site. Search tools can serve a variety of purposes in an e-commerce environment, including:

- error recovery for navigation — sometimes customers get hopelessly lost. Sometimes they search for something they know is there, but the navigation interface won't show it to them. In these and similar situations, they turn to 'search'. Note that navigation can also act as an error recovery mechanism for search engines — for example, when local or inline links to product categories or to related items allow a customer to recover from following a search result that was almost, but not quite, accurate
- an alternative to navigation — navigation is often a better alternative to searching, depending on the information need, and vice-versa. A customer may spend one visit jumping from page to page via links but the next visit using only the search mechanism
- a complement to navigation — most often, the navigation system and search system are used in conjunction. Search might be used to find a book on web programming, then navigational links might be used to explore related titles, then a book review might stimulate a sudden interest in component based programming and it's back to the search engine, and so on.

Despite the importance of searching, the many roles it can play and the fact that users prefer it to navigation, search engines are traditionally poorly designed. As noted above, Nielsen claims that more than half of all users are search dominant. Hurst (1999) reports that e-commerce search engines boast a 56% failure rate.

That's more than one in four customers who cannot interact with a site in their preferred mode.

Hurst characterises the three main causes of search failure as:

- interface problems
- lack of results
- inaccurate or otherwise inappropriate results.

To address these issues, there are a number of simple guidelines that designers should follow in building search tools for an e-commerce site.

Guidelines for Search Tool Design

To begin with, search tools, like any control, should be well labelled and highly visible. Because searching and navigating are interrelated activities, search tools should be available from every page. Likewise, the search tool, its operation and its functionality should remain consistent. Hurst (1999) gives a good example of a search engine that changes in its function midway through the site, causing numerous problems for customers.

Search tools should be easy to learn and use, without instructions. Nielsen (1997c) advises that the default search engine should be as simple as possible, with advanced search features hidden for users who really want to go through the trouble. To build a more usable interface, Hurst (1999) recommends avoiding multipart search engines (e.g. 'Select a Store' and then 'Select a Category' and then 'Enter a Keyword' and then hit 'Go').

Behind the scenes, the search mechanism should be well designed to make sure that the customer is always right by being case-insensitive, performing spelling checks, pluralising and unpluralising terms and filling in related terms, etc. Customers should not be expected to know the exact company label for an item (e.g. they search for 'pup-tent' and fail to get a result because the web store only carries 'two-man expedition tents'), nor should they be penalised for misspelling *Of Miice and Men*.

It is important for designers to realise that customers are visiting a store, not a library, and should not receive a lesson in structured Boolean search logic. In fact, Nielsen (1997c) recommends throwing out Boolean phrasing altogether, since even experienced users tend to use the restrictive 'AND' as a default conjunction. (Nielsen gives the example of telling users they own a dog and a cat, and asking them to find information on their pets.

Most users type in DOG AND CAT rather than DOG OR CAT and get few, or no, results.)

In terms of results, the biggest problems stem from:

- too few results
- too many results
- inaccurate or irrelevant results.

For too few results, Rosenfeld and Morville (1998) offer a simple rule — provide feedback. Not finding anything is one thing, but running into a dead end is unacceptable. An empty results page should offer a variety of options, including links to a browsing mechanism and clickable tools for improving the search. For example, if a customer searches for a 'C174 Power Drill replacement chuck' but doesn't come up with anything, the last thing a company wants to do is sneer at this disappointed individual and say 'expand your search parameters'. Instead, a simple link to 'search for power drills' should be offered.

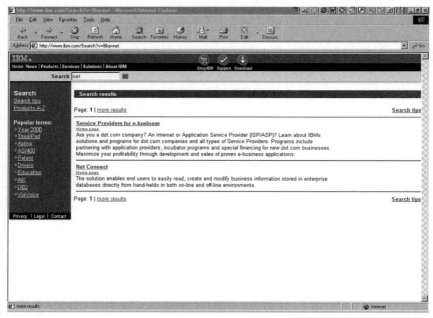

Figure 6.1: http://www.ibm.com (April 2000)

For too many or irrelevant results, Hurst (1999) recommends using key-worded pages. These semi-static HTML pages offer default results with the most appropriate or relevant links and an option to wade into the high volume result list if needed. For example, Figure 6.1 shows a page from IBM which offers customers two key results rather than the customer-unfriendly list of the 110 results that were actually found.

In summary, a search interface should:

- be available from every page
- be simple to use
- be forgiving of variations in search phrases
- offer feedback for failed searches
- offer well organised and easily digestible results.

In addition to the sources referenced above, readers are advised to visit the *C|Net Spotlight on Navigation Design* and *Webreview's* Navigation and Information Architecture sections.

Search Critiques

Based on the guidelines above, it is fruitful to examine search tools 'in the wild'. Figures 6.2 and 6.3 show multipart search tools from CD Quest and Egghead. As noted above, the extra control given by a multipart search is not necessarily worth the added burden placed on the customer. However, if it is used, it should be used in the most customer-friendly way possible.

Figure 6.2: http://www.cdquest.com. Close-up of search tool (May 2000)

The search tool at CD Quest is very limiting for three reasons:

1. It offers four search categories ('Artist', 'Title', 'Soundtracks', 'Song') but does not offer a 'Search All' option, which should not only always be present, but always be set to default. Customers who aren't sure if 'Limping Along' is a song, album or band will need to search three times just to find out it is none of these.

2. The labels for the search categories are very poor and inconsistent. Who is the artist on a compilation album? If a customer searches for 'Camelot' under 'title' will he get a

result? The problem with these labels is that they reflect the logical structure of the database behind the site. No customer should even need to think about this structure, not to mention be constrained by it — the database logic should be transparent to the user.

3. CD Now has forced customers to do the work that the database administrator should do. Customers are required to enter in names in a specific order and to drop leading articles (like 'the'). Assuming anyone even reads these instructions, it is unreasonable for a customer to need to do the work that the company should be doing (not to mention the great dilemma of how to search for albums by the band called 'The The'...).

Egghead's search tool (Figure 6.3), on the other hand, is implemented in a much more customer-friendly fashion. To begin with, the dropdown menu (which offers a choice of the stores or the auctions) also has a default 'Both'. Customers can thus safely ignore the multipart aspect (which many do) and get on with the search. Category browsing is tightly integrated with links to 'Business' and 'Tax' portal pages directly below the search tool.

Figure 6.3: http://www.egghead.com. Close-up of search tool (March 2000)

Furthermore, there are no instructions for customers to ignore. Instead the work of sanitising queries is done by the Egghead staff and Egghead server, as is appropriate. Even though this is a fairly well implemented multipart tool, it is interesting to note that Egghead has since changed it (Figure 6.4).

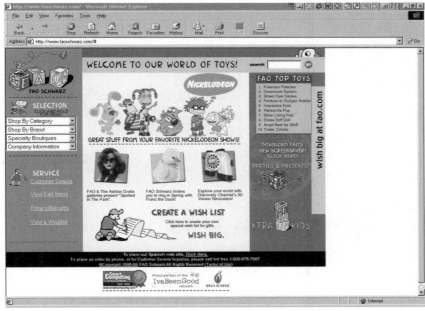

Figure 6.4: http://www.egghead.com. Close-up of search tool (June 2000)

The next examples come from toy stores. Although FAO Schwartz (Figure 6.5) offers an easy-to-use search tool, the visual design makes it difficult to find, especially since the navigation feature (a set of dropdown menus) has a pseudo-search feel to it.

Figure 6.5: http://www.faoschwatz.com (April 2000)

More importantly, the search algorithms used by FAO Schwartz lead to poor results. The second most prominent result from a search for 'dog' is a GI Joe Jungle Fighter, simply because 'dog tags' appears twice in the description. By ranking items based on description, rather than title, the customer is given a totally irrelevant result. On the plus side, FAO Schwartz does what everyone should do — it highlights the searched for word wherever it appears in the results list. This level of context sensitive personalisation is easy and important to implement.

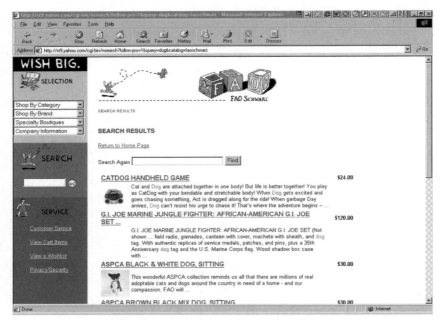

Figure 6.6: http://www.faoschwatz.com (April 2000)

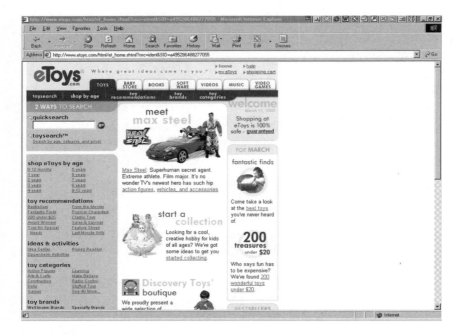

Figure 6.7: http://www.etoys.com (April 2000)

Another toy merchant, eToys (Figure 6.7) does a better job of making the search tool visible by integrating it with the navigation column. As an aside, the navigation feature which, like FAO Schwartz, offers several different arrangements of the site's content is also implemented in a more customer-friendly manner. Since it is just text, it degrades gracefully (FAO Schwartz relies on JavaScript) and since all of the options in each category are readily visible, customers don't need to go hunting.

Figure 6.8: http://www.etoys.com. Close-up of search tool (April 2000)

Unfortunately, eToys makes its search tool hard to use by offering two poorly labelled options, 'quicksearch' and 'toysearch' (see Figure 6.8).

The fact that one of the labels is trademarked hits on the gist of the problem — these are cutesy eToy phrases, not customer-friendly labels. Customers are posed with a choice between an apparently quick search which is desirable (no one likes a slow search) and a toy search which sounds relevant (though confusing — what else is there to search?). eToys customers must have complained and, to their credit, eToys listened. Figure 6.9 shows the new search tool.

Figure 6.9: http://www.etoys.com. Close-up of search tool (June 2000)

While the interface itself has been corrected, the results of the search remain poor, as shown in Figure 6.10 (a search in June 2000 had the same class of results).

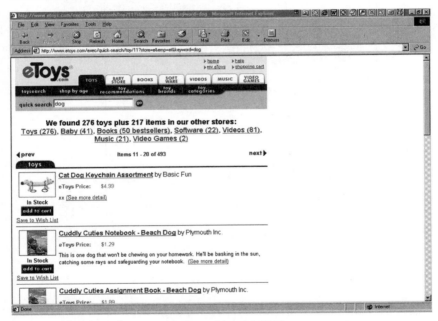

Figure 6.10: http://www.etoys.com (April 2000)

The results page shows nearly 500 items, which are not in alphabetical order, nor grouped by price, nor by age range — in fact, they are seemingly random. A list of 500 items, without structure, is simply not useful to a customer.

Finally, Catalog City is an interesting hybrid business that offers an e-commerce solution for a number of existing mail-order catalogues. The search tool (Figure 6.11) is multipart and suffers from a lack of global default. However, because many customers are searching for shops and not products, the filtering system makes sense. An excellent feature, which is extremely customer-friendly, is a link that resubmits the last search entered by the customer.

Figure 6.11: http://www.catalogcity.com. Close-up of search tool (April 2000)

Although the tool is well implemented, the system does not provide graceful error recovery. With so many vendors and products, it is probably rare that a search yields nothing. But when it does happen, as noted above, the customer-friendly company should take the blame, not pass it back to the customer. Figure 6.12 shows the error page.

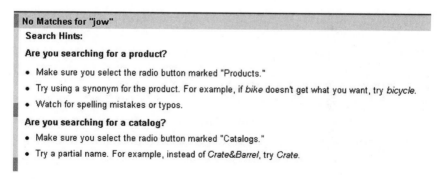

Figure 6.12: http://www.catalogcity.com. Close-up of error message (April 2000)

The list of instructions sent to the customer should be sent as an internal memo to the database programming team. Synonyms for search terms, spelling and partial word matching are all things that the system should be doing, not the customer. If customers do get results, they get a ton of them, and Catalog City handles the volume well, providing filtering and sorting tools to shorten and lengthen the results, sort by price or merchant and so on.

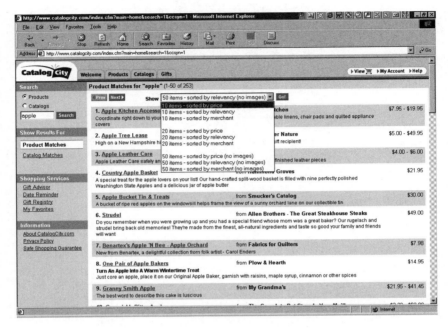

Figure 6.13: http://www.catalogcity.com (April 2000)

To conclude, search tools require customer-friendly design on a number of levels. Interface and page designers must work closely with content providers (who write summary copy, error messages and more) to create tools that are simple and pleasant to use but, most of all, that work. Using a search engine is not a hobby. Customers use the tool to accomplish a goal. The extent to which the search tool helps them accomplish that goal is the true measure of its customer-friendliness.

CHAPTER 7:

Purchasing Interfaces

Products, Shopping Carts and Cash Registers

The two interfaces discussed so far — navigation and search — are primarily used to support the shopping process, which involves research, comparison and decision-making. Once the decision to buy has been made, the customer relies on well designed purchasing mechanisms.

Three primary tools are used for purchases:

1. the product page.
2. the shopping cart.
3. the cash register or check-out page.

The product page does double duty as its content is important to the shopping process as well. As a purchasing interface the product page needs to:

- make it clear what the customer is buying and how much it costs
- make it easy to add the product to the shopping cart and/or to check the cart's contents
- make it easy to get to the check-out counter.

The shopping cart is an information management tool for the customer, which should not only hold the list of purchases but also allow the customer to modify the order and see, at a glance, the total price. The shopping cart should also have two additional pieces of functionality which Hurst (1999) calls critical — links to continue shopping and links to the check-out.

Finally the check-out page itself needs to provide an at-a-glance summary of the order, offer at least as much flexibility as the shopping cart and allow the customer to finish the process in a quick, simple and non-intrusive manner. In fact the shopping cart and check-out pages are the most critical pages in the site, because literally every purchase is handled by these pages.

Guidelines for Purchasing Mechanism Design

Following our guidelines for fast, flexible and usable design, we can formulate a set of design principles for product pages, carts and cash registers.

In terms of speed, although product pages almost always require photos, shopping carts and check-out pages should never be weighed down with graphics. The reason is simple. Product pages are generally static but shopping carts and check-out pages are not, and too much time is already lost in presenting these dynamically generated pages. In terms of flexibility, the functionality of a cart or check-out is key to the success of the store. This means that even if cutting edge and non-standard technology is used elsewhere in the site, these pages must be completely interoperable and accessible. In general, this means keeping as much functionality as possible on the server side and serving mainly plain HTML to the browser.

Making sure the browser doesn't crash is important, but it is even more critical not to break the customer. As noted earlier, whether a purchasing mechanism is well designed or poorly designed boils down to whether the customer is going to be rewarded or punished for deciding to buy. Therefore, the usability of the purchasing mechanism is of great concern. In general, designers should:

- make the 'Buy/Add to Cart' button highly available, highly visible and clearly labelled
- make it easy to reference the check-out page and shopping cart from every product page
- make it easy to continue shopping from the cart page
- make it easy to modify the contents of the cart without instructions
- make it easy to go through the check-out without registering or being asked for irrelevant information.

Purchasing Critiques

In the previous chapter the weaknesses of eToys' result pages (Figure 7.1) were discussed. One of the strengths of this chaotic list is that, should customers find the product they are looking for, the 'add to cart' button and price are immediately available, along with a link to the product page.

This is an important customer-friendly principle: make it easy to buy as early in the shopping process as possible. If a customer has found the item he is looking for, at an acceptable price, there is no need to go further into the site. Egghead, at first glance, provides this tool, but the reality is quite different (Figure 7.2).

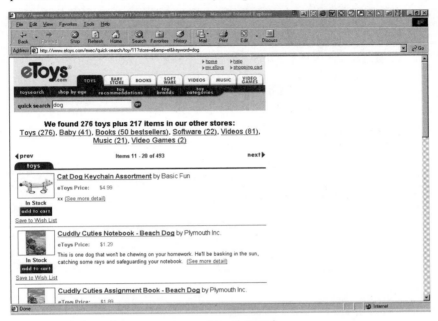

Figure 7.1: http://www.etoys.com (April 2000)

Type	Category	Title	Manufacturer	Price
Buy	Multimedia	3DFX VOODOO 3 3000 AGP2X-16MB SDRAM VIDADPT TVOUT	STB SYSTEMS	$112.99
Buy	Multimedia	A3D ADVANTAGE WAV SC 256-VOICE EQ REVERB EFFECTS	HI-VAL	$22.99
Buy	Desktops	ACERPOWER 4300 DT 6/C500-64MB 6.4GB 40X ETH W98O	ACER	$593.99
Buy	Desktops	ACERPOWER SE MCT 6/C500-64MB 13GB 40X ETH W98 1YR	ACER	$656.99
Buy	Desktops	ACERPOWER SE MCT 6/C500-64MB 8.4GB 40X ETH W98	ACER	$597.99
Bid	Computer Products	ACOMP BOOK PC with Intel Celeron 400MHz, 64MB RAM, 6.4GB HDD, 6X DVD, 56K Modem (New)	ACOMP INC.	$550.00
Buy	Business Software	ADOBE ILLUSTRATOR V8.0 CROMWIN	ADOBE	$400.99
Buy	Multimedia	ALL IN WONDER 128 AGP ATX-16MB WHT BOX	ATI TECHNOLOGIES	$153.99
Bid	Computer Products	AMD Athlon 500-900MHz Epox Motherboard w/ Audio (NEW)	EPOX	$135.00
Bid	Computer Products	AMD Athlon 500-900MHz FIC Motherboard w/ Athlon 750MHz CPU, Cooling Fan - Bundle Pack(New)	CUMETRIX	$399.00
Buy	Home Software	ANASTASIA CROMWINDOWS AND POWERMAC COMPATIBLE	20TH CENTURY FOX HOME ENT	$6.99

Figure 7.2: http://www.egghead.com. Close-up of search results (April 2000)

In this figure, which shows the results of a search, two buttons are conspicuous: 'Buy' and 'Bid'. The product name is available, as is the price — the bare bones information needed to make a purchase decision. But the buttons do nothing. They are, in fact, merely labels indicating whether the item is in a store or an auction. As a result of this poor labelling decision, the interface, and the opportunity for a quick sale, is presented in a decidedly unfriendly manner. This is a classic example of designers ignoring the natural affordances of a web element — buttons invite pushing and verbs, such as 'buy' and 'bid', indicate actionable elements.

Clicking through to a product page (Figure 7.3), the Egghead purchasing system is again delivered in a confusing manner. Nielsen's (2000b) studies have shown repeatedly that customers, in response to sensory overload, have trained themselves to ignore anything that looks like banner advertising. Despite this, the control that allows a customer to add the item to the shopping cart looks like a banner ad. Furthermore, the button that allows a customer to check the cart without adding anything is hard to find because the navigation bar at the top is so busy.

Figure 7.3: http://www.egghead.com (April 2000)

Having added an item to the cart, there are further problems with the implementation. Egghead uses the common method of asking the user to change the quantity to '0' to delete it. (This is not necessarily the most customer-friendly way to go about it. After all, in a 'real' store, customers are free to stick an unwanted item on any shelf close by and let the staff return it to the proper place.) What complicates this mechanism is the fact that the instructions (which again, should not be needed) are buried below the table, away from the control (Figure 7.4).

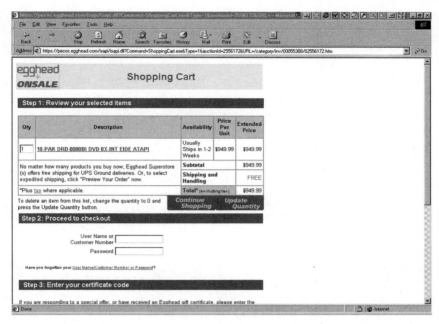

Figure 7.4: http://www.egghead.com (April 2000)

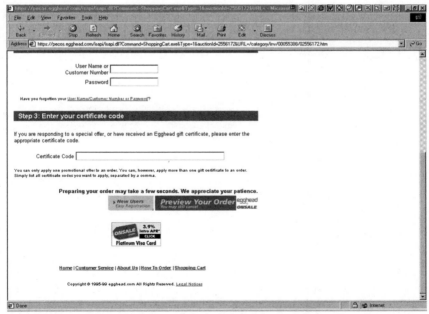

Figure 7.5: http://www.egghead.com (April 2000)

A more serious problem related to the shopping cart is that the 'Step 2: Proceed to Checkout' option is for registered users only. New shoppers are ignored. Registration should not be required to buy, but if it is, the means to register should be highly visible. There was a button to register on the product page, but that was before the customer made a decision to buy. There is a registration button on the shopping cart page as well, but it is at the bottom of the page (Figure 7.5). Also, it again looks like an ad and is sitting on top of an ad, so it is easily ignored.

The registration process itself (Figures 7.6–7) is lengthy, intrusive (requires day and evening telephones, plus email — one of these alternatives alone should suffice), requires that customers opt-out of a junk mail list and requires full credit card information.

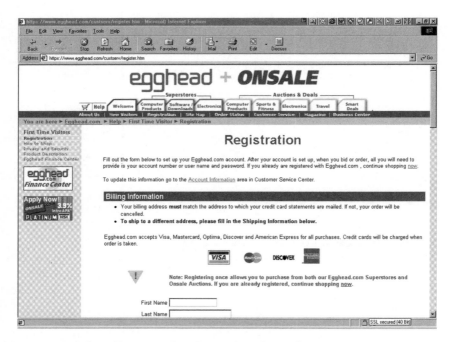

Figure 7.6: http://www.egghead.com (April 2000)

Winnie-the-Pooh is the master of elegant simplicity and in the next example has found an appropriate home. Figure 7.8 shows a product page at KB Kids (Pooh building blocks). KB Kids makes the purchase process painless. The product page offers a conspicuous purchase button and shows a good deal of solid product information (including customer reviews) in a clear manner.

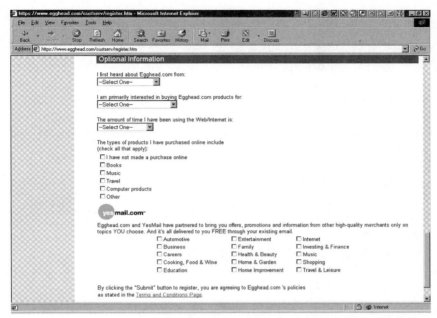

Figure 7.7: http://www.egghead.com (April 2000)

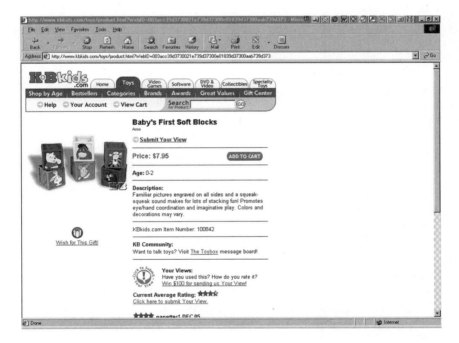

Figure 7.8: http://www.kbkids.com (April 2000)

Once a customer decides to buy a set of Pooh blocks, the shopping cart (Figure 7.9) is one of the most usable I have seen. To delete an item, directly below the quantity box is a button that says 'Delete'. Most importantly, clicking this button immediately refreshes the page to provide feedback to the user that the task was successful. To reflect a change in quantity, there is a button that says, unambiguously, 'Update Quantities'. Again, this offers an instant reload. Here we have clear labels, visible controls and visible results.

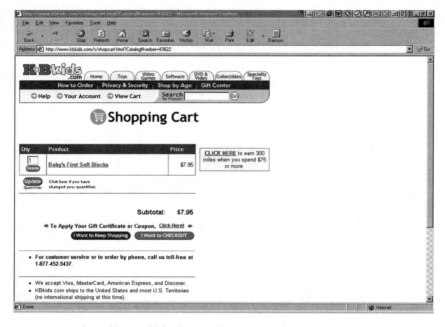

Figure 7.9: http://www.kbkids.com (April 2000)

The two functions that Hurst (1999) said were required for a good shopping cart — links back to the store and links to the check-out — are available and again clearly labelled with two customer-friendly phrases: 'I want to Keep Shopping' and 'I want to CHECKOUT'. Clicking on the check-out button, a customer sees Figure 7.10.

This is a wonderful check-out page. All promotional and distracting content has been stripped away for clarity; privacy, shipping, returns and security are all clearly visible and, most importantly, new and returning customers are given equal treatment.

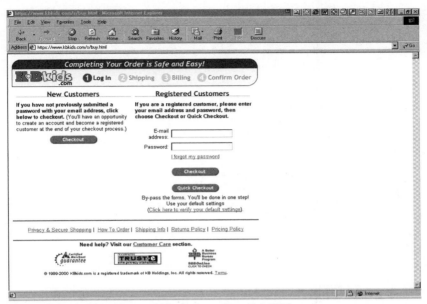

Figure 7.10: http://www.kbkids.com (April 2000)

By far the best quality of the page is not a design feature, but rather a policy decision: 'If you have not previously submitted a password with your email address, click below to checkout. (You'll have an opportunity to create an account and become a registered customer *at the end of your checkout process*.)' This is customer-friendly purchase design. Make it easy to choose an item and easy to change your mind. Make it easy to buy without becoming a registered user. Presented in this order — great experience and then opportunity to register — most customers will. Presented the other way — poor experience and required registration — the result is abandoned carts drifting into cars in the big e-parking lot.

The next example looks at buying a telescope tripod at the Discovery Store, an example used in Chapter 1. Again, the '0 plus update to delete' method is used, but at least the instructions are closer to the action. The last minute personalised recommendation is visible in Figure 7.11, which, as previously noted, is a very solid feature. Finally, both continue shopping and check-out options are clearly visible.

Figure 7.12 shows the updated cart, now that the customer has modified the quantity of items. Note that the 'may we also suggest' ad has been removed. A customer-friendly salesman takes 'no' for an answer.

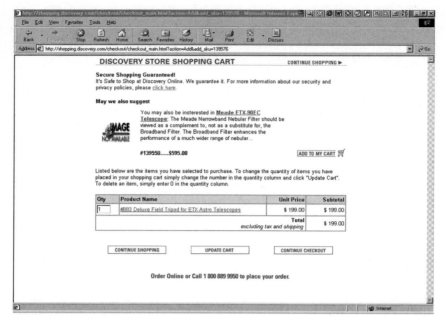

Figure 7.11: http://shopping.discovery.com (April 2000)

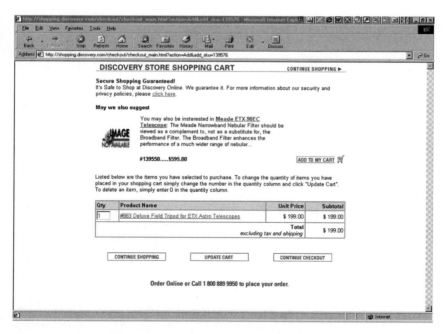

Figure 7.12: http://shopping.discovery.com (April 2000)

Continuing through the check-out process (Figure 7.13), customers are given the option of gift-wrapping the items and filling out a gift card message, both nice features. Like KB Kids, the interface is minimal and easy to use without instructions.

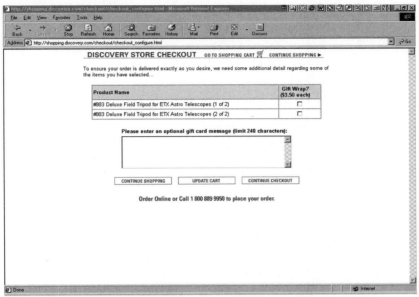

Figure 7.13: http://shopping.discovery.com (April 2000)

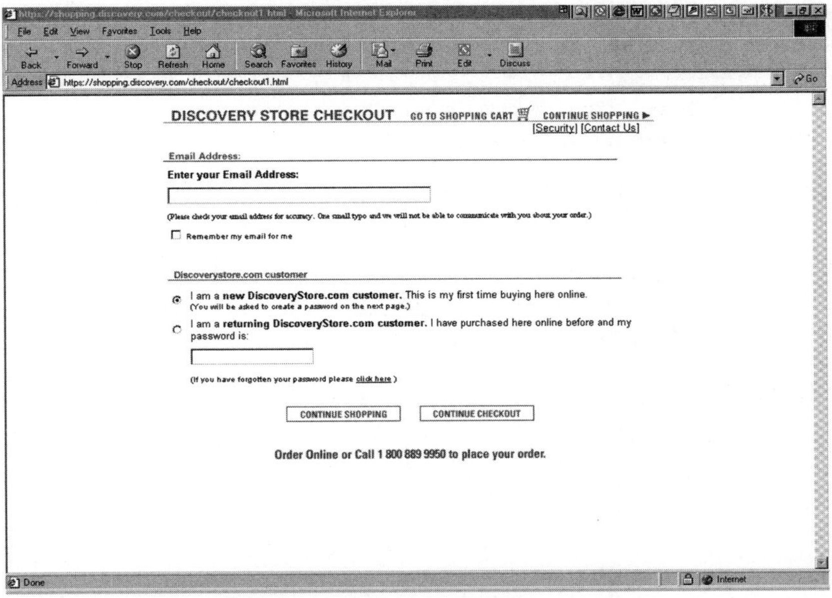

Figure 7.14: http://shopping.discovery.com (April 2000)

Unfortunately, the customer-friendliness ends here. The next page of the process (Figure 7.14) opens the door to compulsory registration which, on top of everything else, is implemented in a confusing manner.

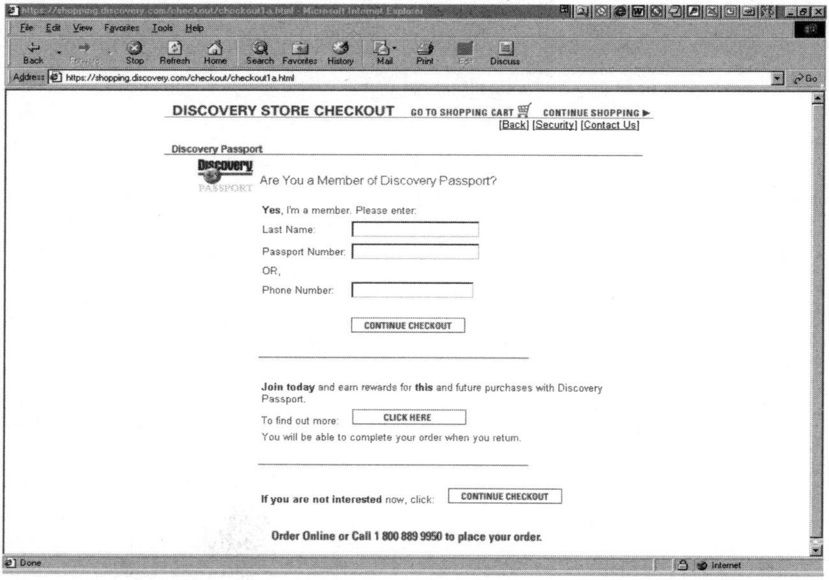

Figure 7.15: http://shopping.discovery.com (April 2000)

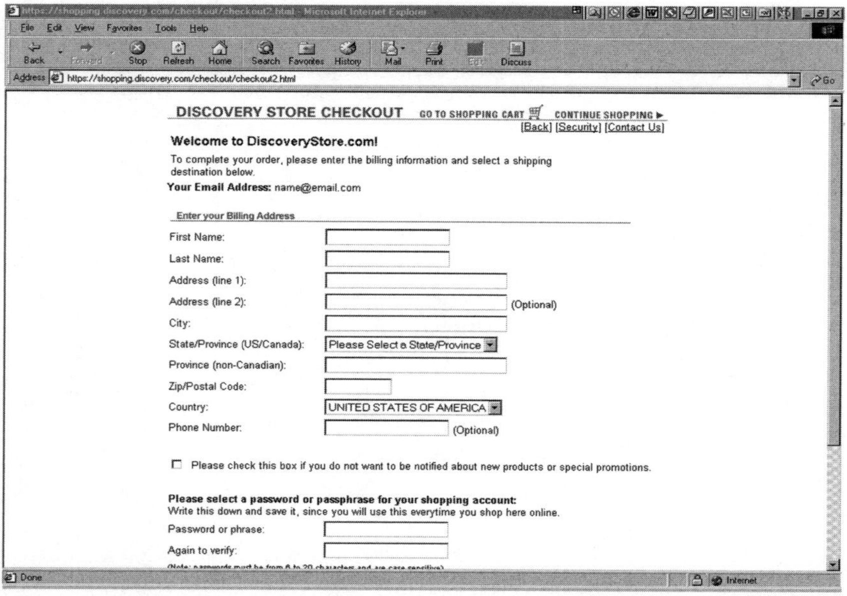

Figure 7.16: http://shopping.discovery.com (April 2000)

The registration page (Figure 7.15) is extremely unfriendly. Customers are asked to become members of 'Discovery Passport', and misled into joining in order to use the continue button which is most prominent. To continue without joining, customers must use a button at the bottom of the page.

Only after solving the riddle are customers given the 'privilege' of filling out the long, unnecessary form shown in Figure 7.16. This purchasing mechanism is all the more disappointing because the experience started so well.

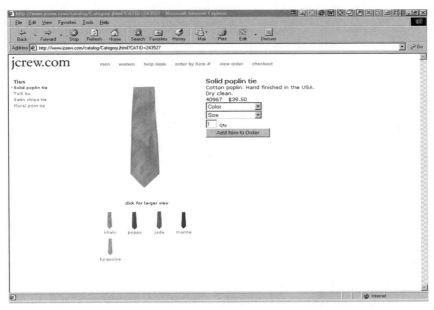

Figure 7.17: http://www.jcrew.com (April 2000)

The final example comes from a company which should deliver rock solid value, since it has been in the distance commerce business for years — JCrew. And, in fact, the purchasing process starts off very strong with a clean, easy-to-use product page (Figure 7.17) that offers a simple mechanism for selecting size, colour and quantity (one of the few shops that allow for multiple selections from the product page). The 'Add to Order' button is the most visible control element on the page, and the 'View Order' and 'Checkout' links appear immediately above the product. The only real negative point is that the dropdown menu for 'size' (Figure 7.18) only has one size. A choice of one is not a choice and customers shouldn't be forced to go through the motions (which they must do if they don't want an error message). The single size should either be defaulted or, better yet, the menu should be removed altogether.

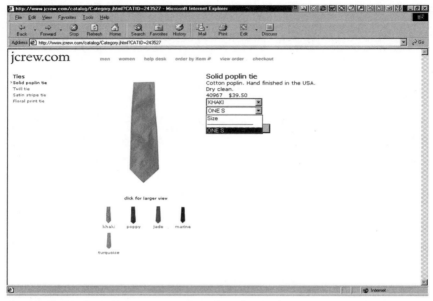

Figure 7.18: http://www.jcrew.com (April 2000)

The shopping cart (Figure 7.19) is good, with a clean table showing all relevant information. The remove function is accomplished with a check box and a button, not as friendly as KB Toy's button on its own, but better than the '0' method. The 'Checkout' and 'Continue Shopping' buttons are clearly visible and appropriately labelled. There is one problem that stands out — a lack of flexibility. Other than removing an item, there is no way on the shopping cart page to change the quantity. This means that customers cannot decide at the last minute to buy an extra tie, or that three ties are too many. When customers get locked into a cart, they tend to abandon it, rather than delete all three ties, find the product page again and order two ties.

Although the interface is strong for the most part, the JCrew order process suffers considerably from server sluggishness. Entering into the secure zone of JCrew's site, I ran into a host of half-baked pages. This kind of server malfunction kills the trust that must exist before a customer consigns his credit card to the network. Figures 7.20–7.22 show three attempts made to load the check-out page before it worked:

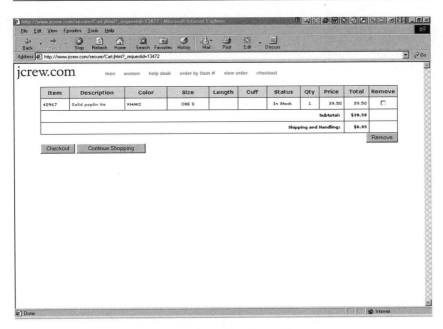

Figure 7.19: http://www.jcrew.com (April 2000)

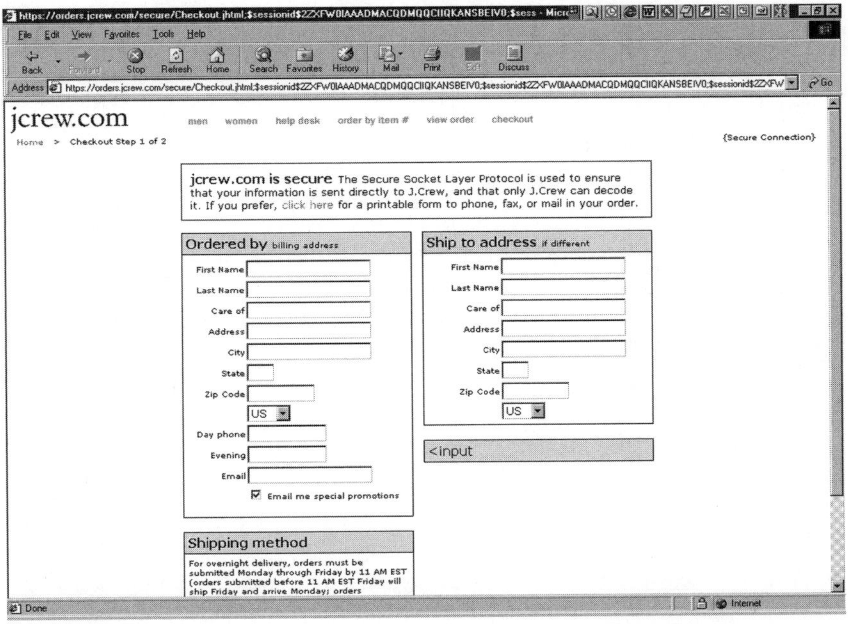

Figure 7.20: http://www.jcrew.com. The check-out page half loads before quitting, complete with a half written HTML tag (April 2000)

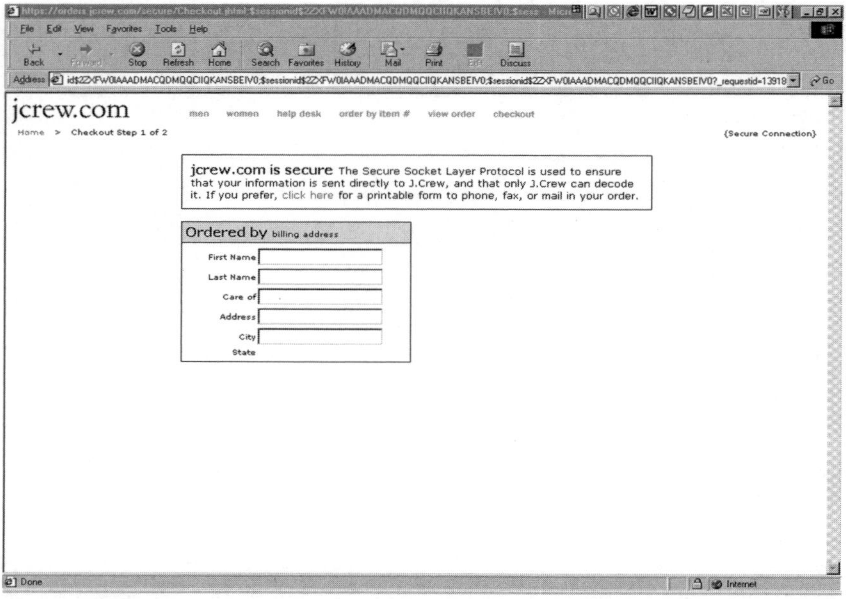

Figure 7.21: http://www.jcrew.com. This time the page doesn't even get a quarter of the way through the process (April 2000)

Figure 7.22: http://www.jcrew.com. All the customer sees is 'jcrew.com is secure The Secure Socket Layer Protocol'. With this level of server failure, how can a customer trust the implementation of SSL? (April 2000)

When the page finally renders (Figure 7.23), there is a 'send as gift' option (always good), an 'opt-out promotional mailing list' (always bad) and a 'redeem coupon' form, which is good, but confusing. For once, instructions would have been appropriate, or at least a label, so the customer would know what to put into this mysterious text field.

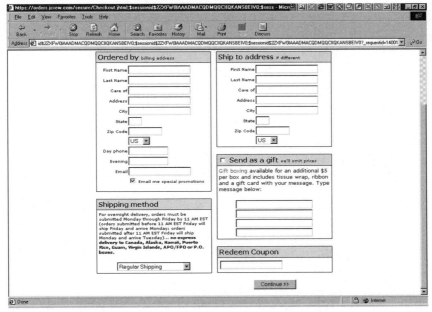

Figure 7.23: http://www.jcrew.com (April 2000)

To recap, every purchase, by definition, goes through the three-part purchasing system of product, cart and check-out. It is critical that these interfaces should be implemented in the most customer-friendly way possible which means:

- fast loading, gracefully degrading, 'no fluff' pages
- usable, visible, clearly labelled control mechanisms with good user feedback
- customer flexibility, allowing for last minute changes
- *demonstrated* respect for customer privacy (when a company tries to trick customers with opt-out junk mail lists, it's hard to believe it cares)
- *demonstrated* reliability and security otherwise the whole system is in question.

CHAPTER 8:

Community Interfaces

The Virtual Community Business Model

Throughout this book I've talked about the web as an environment, an application and an information space. It's important to note that the web is first and foremost a communications medium, a way of connecting people. For this reason the idea of the virtual community (first discussed by Howard Rheingold in 1994) is one of the most interesting and promising business models for e-commerce. Armstrong and Hagel III (1999) write:

> *The notion of community has been at the heart of the internet since its inception ... [But] commercial enterprises ... have been slow to understand and make use of the unique community-building capabilities of the medium ... By adapting to the culture of the internet, however, and providing customers with the ability to interact with one another in addition to the company, businesses can build new and deeper relationships with customers.*

This quote is taken from a short article written in 1996. (The idea was treated in a full-length book, *Net Gain* by Hagel and Armstrong (1997)).

The essence of the virtual community business model is three-fold:

- by allowing users to *publish* and not just *consume* information, and to talk *with* each other rather than just be talked *at* by a company, sites become more attractive
- when customers spend a long time at one site, companies have the opportunity to act as intermediaries between large groups of customers and other companies (group purchasing, very narrow advertising, etc.)
- most importantly, customer created content is usually far more valuable than anything a site can produce.

Virtual communities can come in many forms, but on the web the two most common models are recommendation/review systems and bulletin boards. This chapter offers some guidelines on building interfaces for both types of community.

Guidelines for Community Design

There are three aspects to community design that need to be addressed:

- the interface for registering (if needed)
- the interface for contributing
- the interface for consuming.

Building the registration interface is not so much a design process as a policy-making one. As with the purchase mechanism, it is important that the site respects the customer's privacy — trust is earned over time. And, as with any form based page, labels and clear controls are critical.

The interface for contributing should be seamlessly integrated with the rest of the site, particularly for recommendation systems where there will be a lot of spontaneous posting. 'Running into' a fellow shopper and making a quick comment on a product should not involve interrupting the shopping process unduly. In a bulletin board, navigation between messages and related content management tools need to be designed for maximum usability. Furthermore, they should be unobtrusive — a well placed coffee table facilitates conversation, a poorly placed lampstand interrupts it. Because it is generated on the fly, the interface for consuming information needs to be tightly designed for speed and the structure of the information needs to be clear and flexible (sorting by subject, author, thread, etc.)

In short, like the rest of the site, the community interfaces should be easy and pleasant to use. The attitude conveyed by the company policies will have a tremendous impact on the user's experience. The 'virtual community' is not a bandwagon to be jumped on lightly — playing host is often much more difficult than just selling goods.

Community Critiques

Recommendation and review systems are one of the most common forms of virtual community implemented on the commercial web. They offer tremendously valuable information to retailers, manufacturers and, most importantly, other customers. KB Kids offers a review option that is very tightly integrated into each product page. It is obvious that KB Kids wants customers to contribute, based on the fact that it offers a $100 prize and incorporates the design decision to give the 'Submit Your View' link prominence over even the 'Buy' button!

But why is the recommendation and review content so important? There are four reasons:

- it provides tremendous amounts of data for making stocking decisions
- it provides data on what characteristics of a product make it desirable, thus facilitating copy-writing and promotion
- by cross-referencing products reviewed, lists of products of interest to certain groups of customers can be created, used and shared with customers
- it satisfies customers who enjoy sharing their opinions with an audience of millions.

The interface for drawing customers into the KB community is the product page itself (Figure 8.1), where the link to contribute, and the offer for a prize, are prominent.

Figure 8.1: http://www.kbkids.com (June 2000)

In addition to the review system, KB supports a more private mode of customer-to-customer interaction by offering customers the option of e-mailing a friend about a product. A sample email message is shown in Figure 8.2.

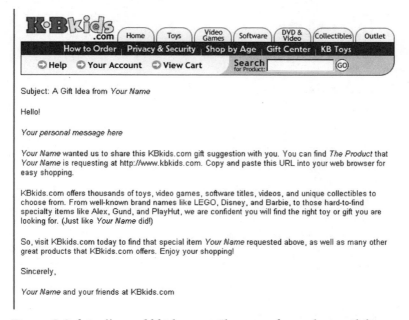

Figure 8.2: http://www.kbkids.com. Close-up of sample email (June 2000)

A sure sign of successful community building is when customers happily send each other ads! Actually, the content of this message is a little crass and beneath the very high standards demonstrated elsewhere on the site. More importantly, a link to the privacy statement (which is on the page, but at the bottom) should always be prominent whenever information is requested.

Customers following the link in order to post a review find a simple, easy-to-use contribution form (Figure 8.3). Like the KB check-out process, no registration is required (although an email address is). Again, a more prominent privacy statement would strongly improve the page, especially since an email address is requested although none appears on the product pages. The obvious question is 'Where do the addresses go?'.

Other than the privacy issue, the form is exemplary; it is easy to use, well labelled and uncluttered. The ranking dropdown menu is very well implemented (Figure 8.4). By combining the star ratings with actual words, the subtleties of the ranking scale are unambiguous.

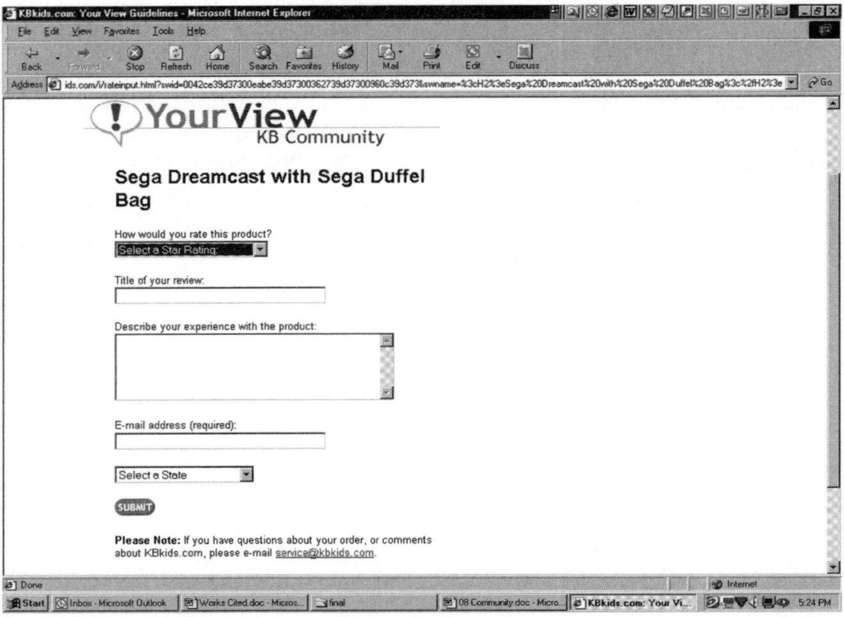

Figure 8.3: http://www.kbkids.com (June 2000)

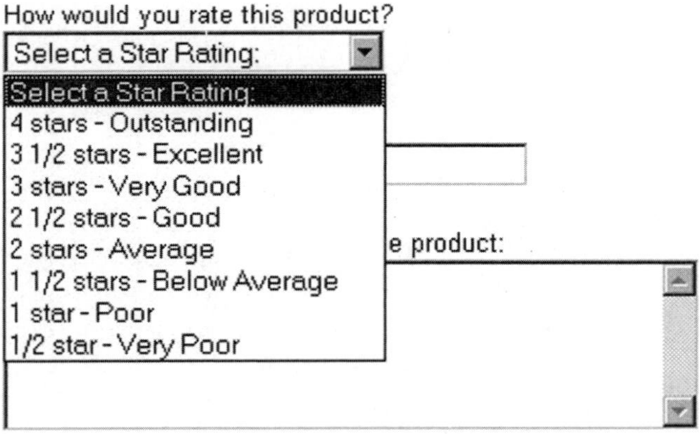

Figure 8.4: http://www.kbkids.com. Close-up of menu in review form (June 2000)

Finally, the reviews themselves are nicely displayed on the product page (Figure 8.5), with the rating summarised at the top — not that most people care about stars.

Systems like these are about the value of human-to-human connection, and glancing at the reviews gives a clear idea that this has been achieved:

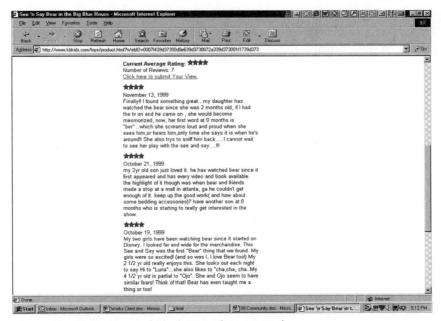

Figure 8.5: http://www.kbkids.com (June 2000)

- 'my daughter has watched the bear since she was 2 months old, if I had the TV on and he came on , she would become mesmorized, now, her first word at 9 months is "ber" ... which she screams loud and proud when she sees him'
- 'keep up the good work (and how about some bedding accessories?) ... have another son at 8 months who is starting to really get interested in the show'
- 'my 2 year old son loves bear and has learned so much from him. This toy is one of few that will keep him occupied for a long time. Thanx for bear and keep him coming!!!'

It is hard to fully appreciate the value of community building even on this small scale — the value to customers who need to hear other parents' real experiences and the tremendous value to companies who, if they are listening, stand to learn a tremendous amount about the market they are trying to serve. Community interfaces are the systems that support what Levine, Locke, Searls and Weinberger (2000) describe when they say markets are 'conversations'.

Amazon.com (of course) pioneered the product review mechanism and has added an excellent twist — a review of reviews. The

need for such a function grew naturally out of the community.
Amazon customers were often debating with each other, rather
than talking about the books! Figure 8.6 shows a page from
Amazon. Every review has a simple question which asks: 'Was this
review helpful to you?' The review is thus ranked: for example,
'14 of 15 people found this review helpful'. It is an excellent
filtering system for customers faced with dozens of long reviews.
It is a powerful pruning mechanism for the Amazon staff (who
can safely delete reviews not valued by other customers).

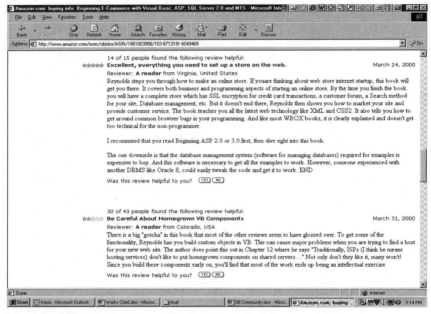

Figure 8.6: http://www.amazon.com (June 2000)

Review and recommendation systems offer community building
on a small scale. Many e-commerce companies go all the way and
offer full-blown bulletin boards. Yahoo! and portal sites like
Yahoo! are in an unusual position in the e-commerce world
because of the enormous range of services they offer. Through
Yahoo! a customer can not only search the web but also set up a
web page, use email, keep address books and calendars online,
chat, use bulletin boards and send instant messages, to give but a
few examples. They can also shop. The Yahoo! shopping slogan
is 'Thousands of Stores. Millions of Products. All with one Wallet.'
To which one might add: 'All in one database'. Cross-activity sites
offer tremendous opportunities but they only work when a site

can maintain critical mass. One of the ways in which Yahoo! stays sticky is by allowing customers to create and participate in clubs.

Figure 8.7 shows the portal page into the Yahoo! clubs. The page is very clean and usable, with a hierarchical directory structure familiar to Yahoo! users and a simple, single field search. It also spotlights clubs with interesting threads of discussion or high traffic volume. 'Getting Started' is prominent and includes a tour feature. The left-hand side of the page displays a personal list of clubs (basically a bookmark function).

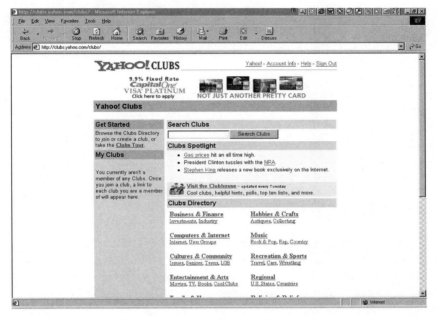

Figure 8.7: http://clubs.yahoo.com (April 2000)

For a collection of information of this size, clean navigation and a good search facility are critical. By offering five different paths into the space, Yahoo! has created a customer-friendly portal into the community. Content management is one of the critical success factors for virtual community building: static content is easy, dynamic content more difficult, but customer-generated content, which is updated by their schedule and not the company's, is a tremendous challenge.

Entering into the tour (Figure 8.8), Yahoo! users will notice something startling: a lack of ads. As a result, the pages are surprisingly easy to digest. Furthermore, the content is well written from the point of view of scannability, the tone is friendly and the functionality offered is empowering and exciting — every customer can create his or her own club.

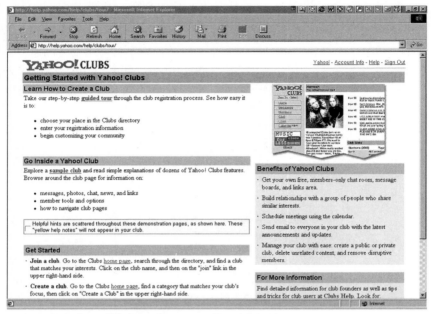

Figure 8.8: http://clubs.yahoo.com (June 2000)

Continuing on the tour (Figure 8.9), the customer is presented with an annotated screen shot of an actual club.

The layout is a little crowded but it works and clicking on the various links will take customers to useful information about the clubs. Using this method, rather than a linear 'how-to' guide, mitigates the inconvenience of a user's manual. However, sometimes the illusion created by this Hollywood 'façade' of a club is shattered, such as when some of the links lead only to an error page.

Inside a real club (Figure 8.10), things are a little more robust. Seen in action, the clubs are impressive and integrate a number of other functions including a private chat room and a list of all users currently online for the purpose of instant messaging. The layout, now without annotation, is palatable, the one ad on the left is unobtrusive (and very well targeted, of course) and the 'Club Stats' section nicely reinforces one of the compelling reasons for joining a virtual community, namely, to be part of something large. The one main flaw in the design — an almost hidden 'Join' button — is well overshadowed by the rest.

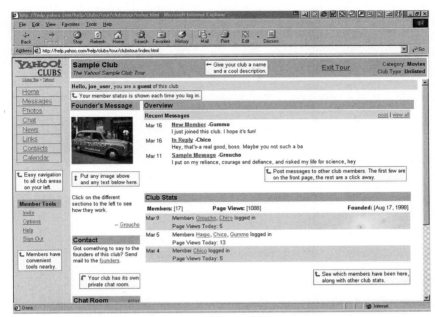

Figure 8.9: http://clubs.yahoo.com (June 2000)

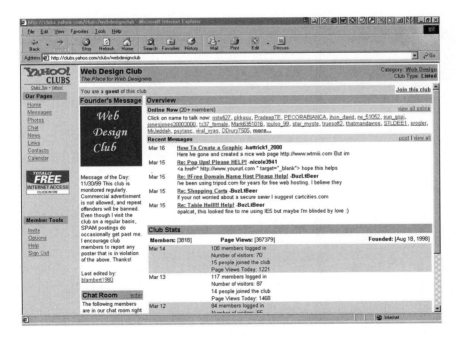

Figure 8.10: http://clubs.yahoo.com (June 2000)

The screens for individual messages (Figure 8.11) are equally well done with a lot of white space, plenty of useful information and good message management utilities. The page supports, amongst other things:

- jumping to specific messages, as well as to the first and last in the series
- moving sequentially through the messages
- responding directly to the poster
- replying to the club
- seeing responses to the message.

Users of USENET will recognise the ancestor of this facility and be amazed at the improvements made.

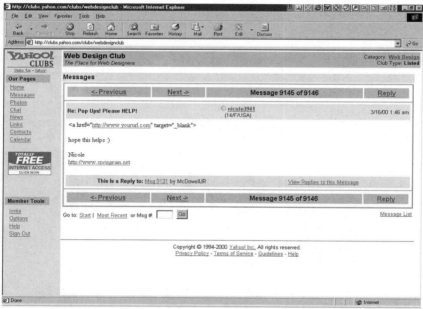

Figure 8.11: http://clubs.yahoo.com (June 2000)

In contrast to the friendly opening of the Yahoo! clubs, I found one of the most successful online communities, Fool.com, to have a remarkably unfriendly beginning. As an Irish user I did not enter in a zip code during registration. The response was:

'Good try. However, we need your zip code please. If you do not have one please enter "none".' This is unforgivably snide and insulting and makes customers feel like they did something wrong, when in fact it was Fool's mistake. This bit of information appeared nowhere on the actual registration page (such as next to the form field). Even if it did, a company would be hard pressed to defend the position that it needs a customer's zip code for the purposes of an online bulletin board. Why not explain politely (and honestly): 'We would like your zip code so we can do some massive data mining down the road ...'!

Getting past the belittling registration process, Fool offers several good features in its service (Figure 8.12), including an easy-to-maintain 'Favourites' function which allows you to track favourite groups, favourite people posting across groups and mentions of favourite company names across groups (Fool.com is an investors' community), amongst others. All in all these features come much closer to simulating the way that people move through social contexts offline.

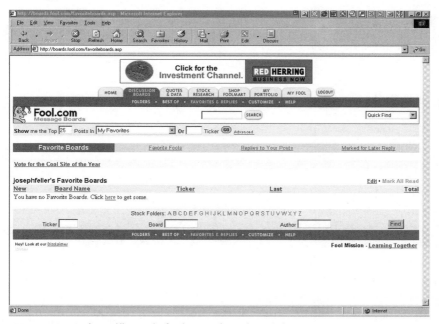

Figure 8.12: http://boards.fool.com (April 2000)

Managing these favourites, unfortunately, can be difficult. The account management tools (Figure 8.13) reflect the complexity of the system, when the goal of good design should be to hide it from the user.

The verbs on the activity centred labels are quite good, such as 'View', 'Edit' and 'Change'. But the nouns suffer. It is not immediately obvious what the difference is between a 'Folder' and a 'Board', for example, or between editing your 'Personal Profile' and changing your 'User Name' and 'E-Mail Address' — isn't that the profile?

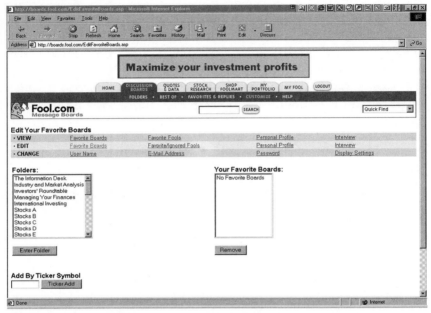

Figure 8.13: http://boards.fool.com (April 2000)

Still, Fool offers one wonderful feature that makes it all worth-while, namely the 'Interview'. One of the hardest parts about participating in an online community is getting started, not with the interface, but with the other people. It's like dropping into a cocktail party of thousands of strangers. Fool offers a terrific ice-breaker and facilitates the building of an online identity beyond user name and email. The 'interview' is non-threatening and begins with 'Answer any, all, or none of the 9 questions below. If these questions don't appeal to you, click here and some of the questions will change.' The fact that there is a bank of questions behind the scenes means that from fool to fool (as the customers are affectionately called), there will be variation in profile. Questions include:

- 'How'd you find out about the Fool? (Make your answer as colorful and truthful as possible.)'
- 'Briefly explain how you select stocks.'

- 'Your most heroic moment in life?'
- 'Describe the worst internet experience you've ever had.'
- 'Describe your fitness program.'

It is valid to ask why I find these questions non-threatening but threw a fit over a zip code. The answer is value: the 'interview' provides a service to customers — it shares value. The zip code is only for the Fool.com. The fundamental design rule for community building is creating value for the *community*.

Which brings this book full circle. E-commerce is the creation and exchange of value using technology like the web. Part of this exchange is tangible — a customer gets a DVD, the company gets a credit authorisation. But much of it is intangible in the form of information, goodwill, 'relationship management' and the rest. No matter what the nature of the value, both customer and company require a cleverly designed, powerful environment in which to actively pursue this unprecedented mode of doing business.

By designing with the customer in mind from the start, by thinking in terms of usage scenarios and by creating robust, scalable information architectures, designers and strategists lay the foundation. By understanding the importance of information and of creating value-adding content; by designing sites that load quickly despite the limitations of the network; by building sites that are platform independent and accessible, and by engineering for usability, designers and strategists communicate to customers a powerful and sincere concern. And by creating flexible, usable and useful systems for navigating and searching, making purchases and connecting people, designers and strategists can deliver exemplary, customer-friendly, successful e-commerce sites.

GLOSSARY

For those readers who may be unfamiliar with some of the technical terms mentioned in the text:

Applet
Technically, an applet is any program which runs inside another program. The most common use of the term refers to small Java programs embedded in a web page and designed to run inside web browsers.

AVI (Audio Video Interleave)
A common file format for video on the web.

Bandwidth
A measurement of how much data it is possible to transmit through a given medium in a given amount of time.

Boolean Logic
A specialised vocabulary embedded in search and programming languages. Uses keywords like AND, OR, NOT, etc.

Cache
In the context of the web, cache refers to local (on the user's hard drive) storage of web content so that additional trips to the web server are not required to retrieve content which has been previously downloaded.

CGI (Common Gateway Interface)
A set of standards for facilitating the exchange of information between applications. CGI programs are "called" by the web server to connect to other programs, such as database management systems (DBMS), and to create interactive web pages.

CSS (Cascading Style Sheets)
An extension to the HTML specification which allows for greater control over the visual display of web content. CSS has several advantages, for example, all pages in a site can share the same style sheet giving a consistent look and feel to the site.

Database Management System (DBMS)

A database is any collection of interrelated data. A DBMS is a program or group of programs which manages the various aspects of a database, such as physical storage, maintaining data integrity, tools for modifying the data, transaction management, etc. Examples include Oracle, SQL Server, Access, and MySQL.

Flash

An animation format which allows the developer to create light-weight multimedia presentations for the web.

Frames

A feature in HTML which allows the developer to split up the web browser's window into several smaller windows, each containing a separate web page.

GIF (Graphics Interchange Format)

A common file format for images used on the web.

HTML (Hypertext Mark-up Language)

The mark-up language used to control the structure and layout of a web page. HTML uses <tags> interspersed with text to format content, embed images, create hyperlinks to other files, etc.

HTTP (Hypertext Transfer Protocol)

The core protocol for the World Wide Web. HTTP controls the way in which data (such as web pages) is exchanged between web servers and web browsers. When a user enters the address of a web page in the web browser, or clicks on a link, the browser issues an HTTP request to the web server. When the server returns the document to the browser, it includes an HTTP header which explains to the web browser what to do with the file.

Intranet

An private network of computers (such as within a company) which uses the same protocols and technology of the internet. The only difference is that intranets are not publicly accessible.

Java

An object-oriented programming language created by Sun Microsystems. On the web, Java is commonly used for writing applets, and has recently gained popularity as a substitute for CGI for linking web servers to other applications.

JavaScript

A language originally created by Netscape Communications. The international standard for the language is called ECMA Script and the Microsoft implementation of the language is called JScript. JavaScript code appears as text in a web page and is interpreted and run by the web browser when the page loads. Its primary uses are creating interactive web pages, managing forms in a web page, and creating "cookies" which allow the web server to "recognise" a user as the user moves throughout the web site.

JPG (or JPEG, Joint Photographic Experts Group)

A common file format for images used on the web.

Modem (Modulator-Demodulator)

Telephone lines are analog (continuous waves of energy) not digital (a string of discreet signals). Modem convert the digital signal of a computer into analog for transmission over phone lines and vice-versa.

Plug-In

An application which extends the functionality of another application. Usually used to refer to the various programs added to web browsers to support the viewing of specialised media types (Quicktime, Flash, etc.).

QuickTime

QuickTime is a video format created by Apple, which in turn supports a variety of media formats.

Resolution

The measurement of a computer monitor screen in pixels by pixels. Pixels is short for Picture Element. The higher the screen resolution, the more screen space available for display. The most common screen resolutions are 640x480, 800x600, and 1024x768.

SQL

The Structured Query Language is a standard language for inserting, manipulating, and retrieving data from a relational database (like Oracle or Microsoft SQL-Server).

SSL
Secure Sockets Layer is a protocol originally created by Netscape Communications. SSL encrypts data to ensure private transmission over the HTTP protocol.

TCP/IP
Transmission Control Protocol/Internet Protocol. This is the core set of protocols used on the Internet. TCP deals with the way data is transmitted and IP regulates Internet addresses.

Web Browser/Web Server
The two core applications of the web. A web browser, like Internet Explorer or Netscape Navigator is used to find, request, and render Web pages (HTML documents and related files). A web server is an application that listens for the requests of web browsers and serves up the documents requested.

Works Cited

AnyBrowser Pages http://www.anybrowser.org/

Apple Computer, Inc. *Macintosh Human Interface Guidelines* (Massachusetts: Addison-Wesley) 1995.

Armstrong, A and J Hagel III, "The Real Value of Online Communities" in D Tapscott (ed) *Creating Value in the Network Economy* (Boston: Harvard Business School Press) 1999, pp. 173-86.

Bahrami, A, *Object Oriented Systems Development* (Boston: McGraw-Hill) 1999.

C/Net Spotlight on Navigation Design, http://www.builder.com/Graphics/NavSpotlight

Cook, J, "Site Optimisation Tutorial" *Webmonkey* (1998) http://hotwired.lycos.com/webmonkey/98/26/index0a.html

Davis, S and C Meyer, *BLUR: The Speed of Change in the Connected Economy* (USA: Warner Books) 1998.

Dougherty, D, "Don't Forget to Write" *Webreview* (1997) http://webreview.com/pub/97/10/10/imho/index.html

Fleming, J, *Web Navigation: Designing the User Experience* (USA: O'Reilly) 1998.

Hagel and Armstrong, *Net Gain* (Boston: Harvard Business School Press) 1997.

Hurst, M, *Holiday '99 E-Commerce: Bridging the $6 Billion Customer Experience Gap* (1999) http://www.creativegood.com/holiday99/

Hurst, M, *Goodexperience.com Update* (2000) http://www.good-experience.com/archives/0200.html

Hurst, M and E Gellady, *White Paper One: Building a Great Customer Experience to Develop Brand, Increase Loyalty and Grow Revenues (1999)* http://www.creativegood.com/creativegood-whitepaper.pdf

Levine, R, Locke, C, Searls, D and D Weinberger, *The Cluetrain Manifesto* (Cambridge: Perseus Books) 2000.

McLuhan, M, *Understanding Media: The Extensions of Man* (Cambridge: MIT Press) 1994.

Meyer, E, *Cascading Style Sheets: The Definitive Guide* (USA: O'Reilly) 2000.

Mulder, S, "Lean and Mean HTML" *Webmonkey* (1998a) http://hotwired.lycos.com/webmonkey/98/43/index3a.html

Mulder, S, "Lean and Mean Tables" *Webmonkey* (1998b) http://hotwired.lycos.com/webmonkey/98/43/index4a.html

Niederst, J, *Web Design in a Nutshell* (USA: O'Reilly) 1999.

Nielsen, J, *Usability Engineering* (Boston: AP Professional) 1993.

Nielsen, J, "How Users Read on the Web" *Alertbox* (1997a) http://www.useit.com/alertbox/9710a.html

Nielsen, J, "Effective Use of Cascading Style Sheets" *Alertbox* (1997b) http://www.useit.com/alertbox/9707a.html

Nielsen, J, "Search and You May Find" *Alertbox* (1997c) http://www.useit.com/alertbox/9707b.html

Nielsen, J, "Who Commits the 'Top Ten Mistakes' of Web Design?" *Alertbox* (1999) http://www.useit.com/alertbox/990516.html

Nielsen, J, *Designing Web Usability* (Indiana: New Riders) 2000a.

Nielsen, J, "Is Navigation Useful?" *Alertbox* (2000b) http://www.useit.com/alertbox/20000109.html

Nielsen, J and D A Norman, (2000) "Usability on the Web Isn't a Luxury" *InformationWeek Online* (2000) February 14 http://www.informationweek.com/773/web.htm

Norman, D A, *The Design of Everyday Things* (Massachusetts: The MIT Press) 1998.

Rayport, J F and J J Sviokla, "Exploiting the Virtual Value Chain" in D Tapscott (ed) *Creating Value in the Network Economy* (Boston: Harvard Business School Press) 1999, pp. 35–6.

Rheingold, H, *The Virtual Community* (1998) http://www.rheingold.com/vc/book/

Rosenfeld, L and P Morville, *Information Architecture for the World Wide Web* (USA: O'Reilly) 1998.

Shapiro, C and H R Varian, *Information Rules: A Strategic Guide to the Network Economy* (Boston: Harvard Business School Press) 1999.

Smith, J, "Effective Writing for the Web" *Webreview* (2000) http://webreview.com/pub/2000/03/10/feature/index4.html

Story, D, "Ten Steps to Effective Web Writing" *Webreview* (2000) http://webreview.com/pub/2000/03/10/feature/index4.html

Strunk, W and E B White, *The Elements of Style* (Boston: Allyn and Bacon) 1979, 3rd edition.

Tedeschi, B, (1999a) "Good Web Site Design Can Lead to Healthy Sales" *New York Times* (1999) August 30.

Tedeschi, B, (1999b) "Seeking Ways to Cut the Web-Page Wait" *New York Times* (1999) June 14.

Tedeschi, B, (1999c) "Real Force in E-Commerce is Business-to-Business Sales" *New York Times* (1999) January 5.

Upsdell, C A, (2000) *Browser News: Statistics, 75th Edition* (2000) February 26, http://www.upsdell.com/BrowserNews/stat.htm

Usable Web, http://www.usableweb.com

useit.com, http://www.useit.com

Viant Design Studio, *Information Architecture White Paper* (1999)
    http://www.viant.com/   press_home_white_papers_experi-
    ence_architecture.html

Web Accessibility Initiative, http://www.w3.org/WAI/

Webreview, http://webreview.com

Web Word, http://webword.com

World Wide Web Consortium, http://www.w3.org

Weinman, L, *Designing Web Graphics.3* (USA: New Riders) 1999.

Zona Research, *Estimated $4.35 Billion in Ecommerce Sales at
    Risk Each Year* (1999)
    http://www.zonaresearch.com/info/press/99%2Djun30.htm